Bunker

S0-DFR-129

GUIDANCE ACTIVITIES FOR COUNSELORS AND TEACHERS

GUIDANCE ACTIVITIES FOR COUNSELORS AND TEACHERS

Charles L. Thompson
William A. Poppen
University of Tennessee

Brooks/Cole Publishing Company
Monterey, California
A Division of Wadsworth, Inc.

© 1979 by Wadsworth, Inc., Belmont, California 94002. All rights reserved. No part of this book may be reproduced, stored in a retrieval system, or transcribed, in any form or by any means—electronic, mechanical, photocopying, recording, or otherwise—without the prior written permission of the publisher, Brooks/Cole Publishing Company, Monterey, California 93940, a division of Wadsworth, Inc.

Printed in the United States of America

10 9 8 7 6 5 4 3 2 1

Library of Congress Cataloging in Publication Data

Thompson, Charles Lowell.
   Guidance activities for counselors and teachers.

   Bibliography: p. 179
   Includes index.
   1. Personnel service in education. 2. Classroom management. 3. Student counselors. I. Poppen, William A., joint author. II. Title.
LB1027.5.T453   371.4   78-31338
ISBN 0-8185-0329-7

Acquisition Editor: *Claire Verduin*
Production Editor: *Fiorella Ljunggren*
Interior Design: *Katherine Minerva*
Cover Design: *Ruth Scott*
Illustrations: *John Foster*
Typesetting: *Instant Type, Monterey, California*

To Our Parents,

Naomi Jones Thompson Katie Poppen
Dr. Charles H. Thompson Alfred J. Poppen

And to

Bettye Alley, Project Director,

and the Project Counselors:

Ethel Benson
Jacqueline Boehler
Mavis Borthick
Henrietta Bradford
Sharon Guthrie
Virginia Neely
Ruth Ann Wilson

PREFACE

Guidance Activities for Counselors and Teachers is based on *Guidance for the Elementary School: Counselor Techniques*, published in 1975 by the Robertson County Board of Education in Springfield, Tennessee, as a final report on a three-year U.S. Office of Education project entitled The Multi-Center Elementary Guidance ESEA III Program. The authors were the project consultants. The techniques presented in the preliminary edition had been researched over a three-year period in seven schools. Only those activities that had proved successful in meeting the project's objectives were included in the book.

Counselors and teachers using the ideas presented in this text are encouraged to adapt the activities to the unique needs of their students. Many of these activities and techniques are appropriate for a wide range of age levels. The preliminary edition focused on methods for attaining the project's objectives of self-concept development, good peer relationships, improved adult/youth relationships, academic achievement, and career development. The present volume retains those portions of the original book that we thought were especially useful. Some of them, however, have been substantially revised and expanded. The book also explores several new topics such as classroom discipline, group guidance and counseling, and in-service education workshop format in reality therapy. In spite of these changes and additions, *Guidance Activities for Counselors and Teachers* retains the practical "how-to-do-it" approach that made the preliminary edition so successful.

We wish to express our appreciation to the Robertson County Board of Education and to Patsy Guenther, ESEA III Director, for granting us permission to use the original book as the basis for the present one. We especially wish to thank Bettye Alley, who wrote and directed the original guidance project and was responsible for pioneering elementary school guidance in seven Tennessee counties. Four of the original project centers now serve as model elementary school guidance programs. In the remaining centers, where local funding was not available for extending the guidance program, several teachers have continued to utilize the methods of the program. Through publications and presentations at national conventions, Mrs. Alley and the project counselors have had a deep influence on guidance programs across the country. We, therefore, wish to thank each of the counselors who participated in The Multi-Center Elementary Guidance ESEA III Program: Ethel Benson, Ingram Sowell School, Lawrence County; Jacqueline Boehler, K.D. McKellar School, city of Milan; Mavis Borthick, Greenbrier School, Robertson County; Henrietta Bradford, White Bluff School, Dickson County; Sharon Guthrie, Central School, Macon County; Virginia Neely, Lipscomb School, Williamson County; and Ruth Ann Wilson, Evans School, Unicoi County. Bettye Alley, Jacqueline Boehler, Mavis Borthick, and Virginia Neely continue to serve as valuable resource persons in elementary school guidance programs.

We are indebted to Jeannette Brown of the University of Virginia, who reviewed the manuscript and offered many helpful suggestions. We are also indebted to Lawrence M. De Ridder, our department chairperson, who granted us released time to serve as consultants to the project. A special thank you goes to our editor at Brooks/Cole, Fiorella Ljunggren, who provided considerable encouragement and help in the completion of this book. Finally, we would be remiss if we did not acknowledge Janice Lee and Janice Stroud for their organization, editing, and typing assistance with the first manuscript.

Charles L. Thompson
William A. Poppen

CONTENTS

APPENDIX A:

APPENDIX B:

APPENDIX C:

Chapter One

ELEMENTARY AND SECONDARY SCHOOL GUIDANCE PROGRAMMING

Since the late 1950s emphasis on guidance in the elementary and secondary schools has been increasing. According to Department of Labor statistics for 1976-1977, over 66,000 people are employed as counselors in elementary and secondary schools. Although the majority of school counselors are employed in secondary schools, there is still a need to increase the number of counselors available to students on the secondary level. An effective developmental-guidance program could easily keep one counselor fully occupied with a group of 30 students. Yet, the counselor/student ratio reported today is approximately 1 counselor for every 420 students.

Hesitancy to employ more elementary school counselors may stem from the unresolved debate about the proper domain and purpose of elementary school guidance. On one side of the debate are those who say that guidance should be primarily the task of a specially trained person and that it should be carried out with individuals or small groups. An extreme opposite position is taken by those who advocate that effective guidance can be best accomplished as a part of good teaching. Although the debate is still going on, it has gradually lessened in the late 1960s and early 1970s, and a different concept for guidance in the elementary school has emerged.

It is now generally agreed by teachers, parents, and school counselors that developmental-guidance programs[1] are needed. The new concept of

[1]The concept of developmental guidance was pioneered by Peters and Farwell (1959).

guidance places less emphasis on remediation and gives more attention to preventing problems in each student's development. Another argument of the developmental view of school guidance is that services are meant for the majority of students, not just for a few with special needs; that is, developmental-guidance services should influence all students in some positive way.

PLANNING CONSIDERATIONS

Guidance practices must be based on the readiness of the students, the teachers, and the community. What ideally *should* be done is no more important a consideration than what *can* be done. Guidance activities that are too advanced for the school and the community will not be successful. Similarly, guidance functions that are beyond the capabilities of the counselors or teachers are better bypassed, and stress should be placed on what the local personnel can do. Thus, ideal practices, existing needs, readiness levels, and resource capabilities all merit consideration.

Guidance programs should be tailored to existing conditions. For example, if direct counseling with students is needed, if the community is ready to accept "counseling," and if a trained counselor is available, counseling services should be provided. If the need is demonstrated for increased involvement between schools and community and if a qualified person is available to work in that area, school/community activities should be stressed. By properly combining knowledge of ideal practices with awareness of community readiness and available talent, unique guidance programs can be developed in elementary and secondary schools (see Figure 1-1).

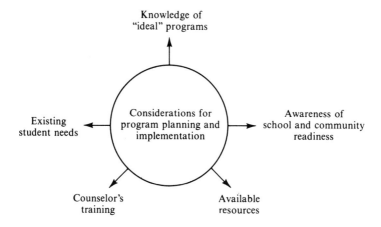

Figure 1-1. Considerations for program planning and implementation.

COMMON AREAS OF EMPHASIS

Most modern developmental-guidance programs share certain areas of emphasis. These areas are listed below and illustrated in Figure 1-2.

1. Developing and improving the student's self-concept
2. Fostering peer relationships
3. Promoting the student's self-discipline
4. Helping parents, students, and teachers improve interpersonal relationships
5. Helping all learners make academic progress
6. Developing understanding and appreciation of the world of work through career-development activities
7. Building effective classroom environments

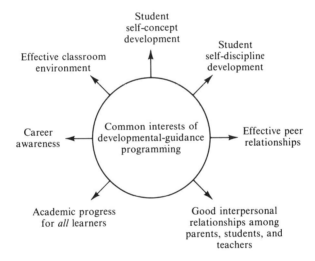

Figure 1-2. Common areas of emphasis of elementary school guidance programs.

Self-concept objectives are pursued through individual counseling, "common-problem" group counseling, developmental-guidance activities, peer tutoring, drug-awareness education, and other planned guidance programs. While older students do participate in self-concept activities, there seems to be more emphasis on self-concept development in the early grades.

Career-awareness activities may vary from counselor-directed short-term (six to eight weeks) units to longer units developed cooperatively by teachers and counselors. In other instances career-awareness activities can be completely integrated into the curriculum and be primarily teacher directed. Field trips frequently highlight career study programs.

Attempts to promote student academic progress may include counseling of parents, in-service education of teachers, consultation with teachers, case-study approaches, peer and volunteer tutoring, study skills units, and attitude reeducation. Counseling and contracting methods are also utilized with students who need academic assistance. Grade contracts are recommended for all classes as a preventive measure for avoiding school failure.

Orientation programs, in-service education, and special "involvement" techniques are all designed to improve interpersonal relationships among teachers, parents, and students. Peer-relationship activities are often the focus of counseling groups, classroom group meetings, short-term units in peer acceptance, and sex education. At times peer-relationship activities are offered selectively to sociometric isolates, while at other times entire classes of students participate.

EFFECTIVE GUIDANCE PROGRAMS

Flexibility and Evaluation

Elementary and secondary school guidance personnel should not only be concerned with objectives and activities that meet existing local needs but also be flexible enough to respond to changing conditions. Some modifications in program objectives should be made as the needs, community readiness, and counselor capabilities change. For example, one year a program might use individual counseling as a means to improve low student self-concept. The following year this same goal could appropriately be pursued by using developmental-guidance activities.

Flexibility and change should be hallmarks of the guidance program but not at the expense of proper evaluation. Each year the objectives for each elementary and secondary school guidance program should be written as behavioral objectives, with specific evaluation procedures. At times a program may have more than one objective in a broad area such as career awareness or peer relationships. The specific activities to be used to accomplish a particular objective should be detailed before the beginning of the school year. Figure 1-3 shows how the objectives can be presented.

Obstacles

The struggles of implementing school guidance programs are not easily detailed on paper. Perhaps it will be sufficient to list some of the primary obstacles in the development of guidance programs. One

Objective	Activities	Evaluation
1. Following a unit on career awareness, the participating students will score an average of 50% higher on a teacher-prepared post-test than on the pre-test.	1. The students will interview their parents concerning their jobs. 2. The counselor will encourage the students to visit their parents' places of employment (if feasible). 3. The counselor will use the Widening Occupation Roles Kit in the classroom as a unit.	1. The counselor will administer the Career Awareness Questionnaire (developed by the counselor) as a pre- and posttest to the participating students.

Figure 1-3. Sample presentation of a guidance objective, activities to accomplish the objective, and evaluation.

extremely serious problem is encountered when some teachers—and in some instances the administrators—have either no awareness of guidance practices or inaccurate conceptions about what school guidance programs offer. The reason for such unawareness or misconceptions may be that these teachers were not exposed to guidance philosophy or practices in their teacher-education programs. It should be noted however that, when teachers and administrators have a guidance "point of view," they are of inestimable value to the program's implementation.

Directly related to the problem we just discussed is the fact that many parents, teachers, and administrators have only a partial idea of what constitutes a developmental-guidance program. Many times a colleague's insistence that guidance is mainly career education or mainly standardized testing impedes the school counselor's efforts to build a fully functioning program. Changing these existing misconceptions about guidance can require an inordinate amount of counselor time.

Staff turnover among teachers, counselors, and other school personnel can be an obstacle to effective guidance practices. Staff turnover extends the time needed to implement a good guidance program. Somewhat related to the problem of staff turnover is the lack of sufficient specialists in related pupil personnel services. Consequently, counselors can be put under considerable pressure to function in the capacity of school psychologists, teacher supervisors, attendance teachers, school social workers, vice-principals, or even clerical workers. When the counselor's functions are extended to these other areas, the focus of his or her attention is often on crisis situations and developmental concerns are of necessity relegated to second place.

Not all of the obstacles have been detailed, because it is almost impossible to imagine the roadblocks that might beset the elementary and secondary school counselor. No matter what these obstacles may be, the successful counselor will find ways for continuing to promote a developmental program.

Results

Here are some positive conclusions drawn by the personnel of the Robertson County Multi-Center Elementary Guidance ESEA III Program during the first three-year period of program development.

1. A successful school guidance program depends on the counselor's ability to coordinate the guidance program with school and community resources.
2. An effective program improves the school atmosphere and results in positive changes in student and teacher behaviors.
3. The best guidance programs are those in which the school counselor demonstrates leadership ability.
4. Schools with effective guidance programs are able to respond quickly to new legislation that requires identification of students with special learning needs.
5. Good materials for guidance and counseling activities help to make a guidance program more effective.

Although it is almost impossible to quantify the combined effect of a school counselor's work, it is important to quantify and qualify as many counselor functions as possible. The public prefers guidance programs that have identifiable activities that account for a better educational experience for all students.

No longer must guidance and counseling activities be supported merely because they make students or teachers feel better; rather, they can be supported because they help people do better. The use of behavioral objectives makes at least a part of the guidance program observable. Certainly many of the effects of guidance programs are intangible, but many are also tangible and open to evaluation. The Robertson County Multi-Center Project showed that beneficial guidance programs can be maintained whenever school personnel and parents develop their own guidance objectives, agree that the objectives are worthwhile, and determine the results of the activities used to reach each objective.

Chapter Two

SELF-CONCEPT DEVELOPMENT

Self-concept, or how a person feels and thinks about himself or herself, is perhaps the central concern of school guidance programs. Students trapped in failure cycles may seek feelings of self-worth through antisocial behavior or through rather extreme forms of withdrawal.

The question for teachers and counselors is "How do we break the failure cycles and self-defeating behavior patterns of those students seeking their identity and self-worth through irresponsible actions?" Writers on human behavior — including Freud, Maslow, Frankl, and Glasser — agree that life goes well for those of us who manage to keep work activities and interpersonal relationships in order. In other words, if, because of the good and helpful things we do for ourselves and others, we feel and think that we are worthwhile people, we are well on the way toward developing a healthy self-concept. But achievement is not enough. A second important aspect of positive self-concept development is the feeling that someone cares about us. And, if this someone is a person with whom we have a sharing and caring relationship, our self-concept will rest on a firmer foundation. When we are able to find more than one avenue of achievement and establish more than one caring relationship, we avoid the dangers inherent in trusting our self-esteem to the success or failure of one given task or one personal relationship.

A young person's self-esteem can be shattered by one low test grade or by one broken friendship. Teachers and counselors are quite aware of this problem because they often find themselves helping students pick up the pieces. It follows that school personnel would want to develop a guidance program that facilitates self-concept development through student achievement and interpersonal relationships. The following guidance-program activities are directed toward helping students increase their feelings of worth and develop more interpersonal relationships. Generally the two objectives go hand in hand because, as students begin to achieve more, they are more likely to establish relationships with other students. When we achieve, both we and others find ourselves worthier of love and respect. This principle seems to also work in reverse. As we develop caring relationships, our achievement is positively affected, particularly when such relationships are based on unconditional love and respect. In sum, self-esteem depends on knowing that someone cares about us and on being successful in our environment.

INDIVIDUAL APPROACHES FOR BUILDING SELF-ESTEEM

Activity: Individual Counseling

Level: Grade K-Adult

Purpose: One purpose of individual counseling is to examine how students develop low self-esteem. The difficulties involved in working with these students have a direct relationship to three of the four life positions outlined in the transactional-analysis approach to human behavior.

1. *"I'm not OK — You're OK" position.* Here the student is saying "I'm no good; I'm stupid, incompetent, and ugly" or making other self-belittling comments such as "John always does better than I do" or "Most people think I'm no good. I haven't asked them, but I know that's what they think."
2. *"I'm not OK—You're not OK" position.* This situation involves distrust between students and teachers or parents. The student may say "I will probably do poorly on the test, and my parents will really be disappointed in me even though I tried to do my best."
3. *"I'm OK—You're not OK" position.* This life position focuses on blaming others for things that don't work out as desired and for one's own faults. The student is likely to say "If it weren't for you, I could do better."

Successful individual counseling should result in attaining the desired

The feeling that someone cares is an important factor in the development of positive self-concept.

(and desirable) fourth life position: "I'm OK—You're OK." People in this position say "I'm an OK person regardless of how well I compete with my peers. My self-worth is not based on my level of achievement. It is desirable to do one's best, but I'm not required to be perfect. When things go wrong, I am willing to accept my share of responsibility and consequences."

Procedure: Two counseling approaches are well suited for the self-belittling student—reality therapy and rational-emotive therapy.

Reality therapy as developed by Glasser (1965) offers a practical guide to building responsibility in students who have chosen to act in irresponsible and otherwise unhelpful ways. Responsibility is defined as trying to meet one's own needs without infringing on the rights of others. The reality-therapy approach confronts students with their behavior and the consequences of such behavior. In brief, the steps are:

1. Become personally involved with students, communicating that you really care about them and hold a positive view of human nature. This is accomplished by listening to students, by withholding judgment, and by confronting them with their own judgment of their behaviors. *Encouragement, support*, and *reinforcement* for honest improvement are other ways to build rapport with students who have low self-esteem.
2. Have students describe their behaviors and what they have been doing

to solve their problems. When students are behaving in unhelpful ways, it is useful to ask them "What are you doing?"

3. Have students make a value judgment about their own behaviors. Ask them "How does what you are doing help you?" and "How does it hurt you?" Probably very few of us change what we are doing until we first conclude that it is not helping us. Sometimes it is advisable to ask questions in specific terms. For example: "How does what you are doing help you learn your math lesson?" "Is what you are doing responsible behavior?" "Isn't your behavior against the rules?" or "Is your behavior in touch with reality?"

4. If students agree that what they are doing now is not helpful, ask them to suggest alternative behaviors that may be helpful. During this step, students are encouraged to brainstorm and to withhold evaluative comments until a list is completed.

5. Ask students to commit themselves to trying one of the alternative behaviors and to report the results of their attempts. Frequently these student plans are drawn and signed as contracts. In other cases verbal plans are accepted; for example, two fighting students may be asked to sit down alone and, without consulting each other, formulate a plan for staying out of fights on the playground.

6. Accept no excuses when students do not meet their commitments. Simply ask them "What are your plans for completing your contract?" If the contract proves to be too ambitious, tear it up and write a new one.

7. Administer no punishment. Students who suffer from failure usually receive enough punishment from the logical consequences of their behaviors. Instead, make sure that the students do understand the consequences of their actions.

8. Refuse no student requests! Instead of coming out with a flat "No!" simply state the conditions under which the request could be granted. For example: "Will you give me 3000 dollars?" "Yes, for a new ski boat and motor that will go 40 miles per hour." Or "Will you do my math problems for me?" "Yes, if you will put my name on your paper instead of yours and pay me one dollar for each problem I do." Of course, legitimate requests can be granted without any special conditions. Stating conditions for saying yes to unreasonable requests is one way of avoiding power struggles and also a way to begin planning how to meet the conditions.

9. Never give up. At least, work with your students longer than they think you will. Positive results may take two months or more.

Rational-emotive therapy as developed by Ellis (1969) offers a system for helping students examine their self-thoughts or self-messages influencing their self-concepts, which in turn affect their personal achievement. Ellis argues that the same events happen to all of us but that a hundred people may react in a hundred different ways to the same event and hence develop a hundred different degrees of feeling about the event. For example, when the teacher asks Mary Ellen to recite something and she can't do it, she may tell herself one of two things: "I failed to recite, and this is absolutely awful. I'm a failure" or "I failed to recite, and this is very unpleasant. I don't want this to happen again, and, to make sure that it doesn't, I will be prepared for each class." The first self-message will probably lead to such feelings of depression, low self-esteem, and nervousness that Mary Ellen will fail again the next time she is asked to recite. The second message, instead, will probably stimulate Mary Ellen to prepare for classes. Although she feels disappointed about the experience, she is not devastated by it.

The counselor employing a rational-emotive approach to counseling would assist students in changing their self-messages to messages that promote positive action rather than self-effacement. The rational-emotive process may start with an examination of the bad feelings being experienced, followed by a report of the precipitating event. Then the counselor asks the student to verbalize the messages that he or she is telling himself or herself about the event. The counselor attempts to illustrate the irrationality of those messages that dramatize the situation. For example, the counselor may ask Mary Ellen how one failure makes her a failure for life or whether she knows anyone who has never made a mistake. Once the irrational message is exposed, the counselor will attempt to help Mary Ellen compose a more sane message, such as the second message above.

Counselors find both the reality-therapy and the rational-emotive approaches helpful in counseling students. Both approaches are easy to learn and apply. Students respond somewhat better to the behavior confrontations and commitment contracts used in the reality-therapy approach. Teachers, too, find the reality-therapy process useful in the classroom. Counselor methods based on reality therapy and rational-emotive therapy can also be used in group counseling.

GROUP APPROACHES FOR BUILDING SELF-ESTEEM

Activity: Classroom Meetings

Levels: Grade K-Adult

Purpose: One of the major objectives of school guidance programs is to use classroom activities to improve the student's self-concept. The technique most often used to achieve this goal is William Glasser's (1969) classroom meeting. Three kinds of meetings are used: social-problem solving, open ended, and educational diagnostic. All meetings have the same basic structure: (a) clarifying a topic completely, (b) personalizing the discussion, and (c) challenging the students toward new thinking and action. Enrichment of the meetings comes from the values-clarification activities suggested by Raths, Harmin, and Simon (1966) and from the developmental-guidance experiences of Moy Gum and others from the University of Minnesota (see American Personnel and Guidance Association, 1973). See Chapter Nine for further discussion of classroom meetings.

The rationale for using classroom group meetings to enhance student self-concept is to:

1. Allow students who have low status among classmates to contribute to class discussion and thereby improve their status,
2. Allow students to realize their "power" by influencing the thoughts and actions of the group,
3. Provide a new type of activity that could become a success experience for many of the students,
4. Allow teachers to see their students engaged in a "new" activity and consequently recognize student potentials and abilities more fully,
5. Allow teachers to learn what is relevant to the students.

Procedure: *Social-problem-solving class meetings* focus on all problems concerning the class as a group and any individual in the class. Typical issues are truancy, teacher/student relationships, and even home problems. The leader of the meeting avoids being punitive and judgmental, since the classroom meeting provides the opportunity for students to judge their own behavior. The discussion is directed toward solving the problem, and the solution should never include punishment or fault finding. Classroom meetings are better if everyone is seated in the front row. The best way to accomplish front-row seating for all is to put everyone in a large circle. Incidentally, why not keep the classroom this way all the time?

Open-ended classroom meetings, described by Glasser as the cornerstone of relevant education, should be used often. They offer students the opportunity of bringing up and discussing thought-provoking questions related to their lives — questions that more often than not can be related to the class curriculum. The magic of the open-ended discussion seems to lie in the fact that for once the teacher is specifically not looking for factual answers. The focus is some distance beyond the memory level of learning. Generally open-ended discussions generate questions and answers demanding analysis, synthesis (creativity), and evaluation skills.

The discussion can begin with the teacher or counselor posing the question "What is interesting to you?" One second-grade class went from a discussion on eyes and what we see with our eyes to what it might be like to not see and finally to how a blind person could read. Because the children were functioning in the concrete stages of cognitive development, it was necessary to have the students experience the limitations and possibilities of being blind. For example, when the discussion became blocked, the teacher ran an experiment to see whether one of the children, holding a coin in each hand, could identify with his eyes shut which was a quarter and which was a nickel.

Open-ended discussions might also explore "what if" situations like those found on many tests of creativity. For example, the class could discuss what would happen if "we were all born the same color," or "all but the highest mountains were covered with water," or "we all had plenty of money and didn't have to go to school or work," or "people everywhere refused to fight in wars even though their leaders ordered them to fight."

Educational-diagnostic classroom meetings are directly related to what the class is studying and can be used to find out how much students already know about a subject or how much they have learned from studying it. Another purpose of the educational-diagnostic discussion is to examine the depth of the students' knowledge. It is easy to test memory level without investigating whether a student can explain the reasons behind his or her "right answer." An effective discussion leader should withhold value judgments. The purpose of the educational-diagnostic classroom meeting is to find out what the students really know and understand. Therefore the students need to feel free to express their thoughts without fear of ridicule or low grades. Classroom meetings are not for grading! In one educational-diagnostic classroom meeting the class discussion went from "What is the Constitution?" to "Does it exist?" to "Do these rights pertain to you?" to "What if you do something on your own property that is against the law?" Some teachers have utilized the discussion format to improve the classroom learning situation by asking their students "What would you do if you were the teacher?" Students enjoy being the teacher if they are free to experiment with their own ideas.

These classroom meetings are most effective when they are an integral part of the regular school program. Elementary school children could have them once a day for 15 to 20 minutes. The classroom meeting is a major procedure for implementing Glasser's (1969) concept of *Schools without Failure.* Can you think of a better way to build self-esteem than to eliminate failure experiences in group discussions? Classroom meetings offer students the opportunity to explore those questions whose answers cannot be found in textbooks or encyclopedias. For example, if you look under *pollution* in the dictionary, you will find a good definition but nothing else. Even the most comprehensive encyclopedia doesn't tell you what you can do to fight pollution in your own area. Answers to problems of world peace, human relations, inflation, shortages of natural resources, and moral dilemmas—just to cite a few—are not available in books of knowledge. Classroom meetings help students learn the problem-solving skills necessary for dealing with these issues. The meetings seem to work best when the following guidelines are used:

1. Identify topic clearly: The question for today is _____. or Can someone restate what we will discuss today? or Today we can discuss _____ or _____. Which will it be?
2. Ask for definitions: What do you mean by _____? What is _____?
3. Ask for specifics: What else do you need to know about that? Tell me more about _____.
4. Ask for personal examples: Do you know anyone who uses _____? Do you ever use _____? How does _____ relate to your life?
5. Ask for agreement: Are there students or teachers who agree with you? who disagree with you? If so, why?
6. Ask for value judgments: What is your opinion about _____? Are you in favor of _____, or are you opposed to it? Why?
7. Challenge the group: How can you find out more about that? Would you like to study that topic or idea? Present hypothetical situations involving the concept: What would happen if we did not have _____?
8. Withhold judgment of right and wrong about the student's answers and opinions.
9. Ask no questions that you would be unwilling to answer yourself. Each student, as well as the teacher, does have the right to pass on any question asked.
10. Remember that answers to questions calling for personal opinions are always right for the person expressing the opinion. One of the things students learn from classroom group meetings is that opinions are to be respected even when one doesn't agree with a particular opinion. It is important that students feel OK about valuing something that the majority of the others don't value.
11. The nine steps proposed in the reality-therapy counseling model, which we discussed earlier, are also effective in classroom meetings when the group is trying to solve a particular problem. Especially important is the step concerning student commitments.
12. As we said earlier, the group seems to work best when the students sit in a circle, so that everyone can see everyone else. The teacher or counselor can facilitate group discussions by encouraging members to talk with each other rather than through the teacher—a new experience for those teachers and students who have been accustomed to teacher-child-teacher-child communications patterns.

The following checklist is included for teachers and counselors who wish to evaluate their group-leadership skills in classroom meetings.

Group-Leadership Checklist

____ Leader has series of questions about topic to be discussed.

____ Participants are seated in a circle, so they can establish eye contact.

____ Leader stops side conversations.

____ Leader sits in a different place each meeting.

____ Leader discusses purposes of meeting.

____ Meetings adhere to time limit.

____ Leader is relaxed, and participants are at ease.

____ Leader sets topic: The question for today is _____. *or* Can someone restate what we'll discuss today?

____ Opening is stimulating (evaluation is based on participants' responses).

____ Choice of topic is frequently given to the class: Today we can discuss _____ or _____. Which will it be?

____ Leader is nonjudgmental.

____ Leader does not offer solutions.

____ Leader tries to stimulate nontalkers by looking for nonverbal cues.

____ Leader asks for personal examples: Do you ever _____? Do you know anyone who _____?

____ Leader calls for agreement/disagreement: Do you know anyone who agrees with you? disagrees with you?

____ Leader doesn't interrupt to correct bad grammar or object to profanity. However, leader does ask students to evaluate what profanity does for them.

____ Questions challenge participants at their own interest level: How can you find out more about that? Would you like to study that topic or idea?

____ Most questions can be answered by participants.

____ Leader redirects group to topic.

____ Leader frequently asks participants to clarify their ideas.

____ Leader uses "listening games" to build and maintain listening skills.

____ Leader asks participants to evaluate meetings.

____ Leader eliminates topics and questions that students don't evaluate highly.

____ Leader asks participants to develop new topics.

____ Leader doesn't allow a participant to be belittled or threatened by other group members (no destructive comments allowed).

Activity: Feelings Classes

Level: Grades K-8

Purpose: The main purpose of feelings classes is to give attention to the affective development of students. More specifically, feelings classes focus on five main ideas:

1. Many kinds of feelings exist.
2. Nearly everybody experiences all these different feelings.
3. It is alright to have these feelings.

4. Having a feeling is different from expressing a feeling.
5. There are ways of expressing one's feelings that are not harmful to others and that are often even helpful.

Love, hate, fear, anger, and joy are very normal human emotions that affect the way people learn and develop. We must, therefore, learn to accept these feelings in ourselves and in others. However, we also need to learn "helpful" ways for expressing these feelings—ways that don't infringe on the rights of others and don't block personal growth and development. It is also important that we are aware of the feelings of others and that we know how to react to such feelings.

In an age too often characterized by violence and aggression, we would do well to begin early in our efforts to assist children to understand the meaning of accepting and expressing feelings, especially negative feelings. One of the most valuable contributions we can make to a child's education (in the broadest sense of the word) is to nurture the concept that feeling any feeling is OK but that all forms of expressing that feeling are not OK. Feelings classes offer a useful avenue for making such contributions.

Procedure: The counselor or teacher can plan activities that help students learn and understand the feelings-class concept. The following group activities were utilized by project counselors for consciousness raising as well as discussion stimulation.

1. "Feelings buttons" have been utilized in the elementary school grades to help children realize that several types of feelings exist. These buttons can depict facial expressions (for example, a happy face) or describe in a few words a particular feeling. The children wear buttons that indicate their feelings at the moment.
2. Writing lessons may include keeping a diary of the feelings the children have each day, why they had the feelings, and what they did about them. Even an arithmetic lesson can relate to the topic of feelings. A "feelings pie" drawn by the student and divided into parts representing the way the child feels most of the time combines fractions and emotions. For example, a student may choose to divide his or her pie into 1/2 happy, 1/4 sad, and 1/4 frustrated.
3. During art class the students can draw or paint expressions of feelings. For example, most students enjoy drawing the Peanuts cartoon characters, who so effectively depict such a variety of feelings.
4. Snapshots, pictures of the students as babies, and magazine pictures showing various expressions of feelings may be shared. The pictures can also be used in bulletin-board displays created by the students.
5. Some classrooms have a "feelings pillow" or a punching bag available for the venting of hostile feelings.

6. Role playing and creative drama offer effective ways of learning how to express feelings. Students may role-play characters in a play, other students in the class, or people they know outside of class. The best way to create empathy for another person's situation is to let someone role-play that person. Role playing can also be useful in working out personal conflicts with fellow students and adults.

7. Learning about the expression of feelings also means learning that it is normal to feel hate toward certain individuals at times but that one cannot express this hate by hitting people with a ball bat. It is OK, however, to draw pictures of the individuals in question, tape the pictures on the punching bag, and then beat the bag with the bat.

8. Students in the middle-school age group respond well to discussions of how to change bad feelings and what to do about feelings of depression. Students may be asked to describe what they are experiencing and what is happening to them because of their feelings and consequent behavior. Can there be a change in feelings without a change in behavior? How does the feelings-behavior connection work in your life? Can you get rid of a bad feeling without changing your behavior? If so, how? Questions such as these can facilitate group discussion on the topic. Group feedback to each member serves as a mirror of how he or she affects others with his or her expressions of feelings and behaviors.

Ellis (1969) takes issue with some of the objectives of feelings classes. He writes that there is danger in concentrating too much on the expression of hate and anger. Support for this view comes from research findings showing that the expression of anger seems to increase rather than decrease the frequency of angry behavior.

If, indeed, anger begets anger, we might want to examine more closely the things we tell ourselves that make us get so angry in the first place. Why do two people react so differently to what appears to be the same stimulus event? Certainly part of the answer lies in what each person tells himself or herself about the event. For example, Tom and John are standing in the cafeteria lunch line. Harold arrives on the scene and pushes in ahead of both boys. Tom tells himself "I'm annoyed with Harold for crowding into the lunch line, and I'm going to talk to him about it." Before Tom can talk to Harold, however, John, who has been telling himself something quite different about the incident, has already taken action: "He can't get away with crowding in ahead of me in the lunch line. He's trying to make me look bad in front of the whole school, and that's really awful. Well, he's gone too far this time!" Bang! John hits Harold, and soon both boys are scuffling on the floor. The fight continues until broken up by a teacher who sends them to the principal.

Without negating personal feelings, it may be helpful for students to focus their attention on what happens at point *B*, between point *A*

(Harold's crowding in) and point *C* (John's punching Harold). At point *B*, one usually has the option of saying one of two things: (a) "I don't like Harold's crowding in front of me. I wish he wouldn't" or (b) "I can't stand Harold's crowding in. That's absolutely terrible!" Students can explore the nature of their self-messages, which can make them feel extremely depressed instead of disappointed or extremely angry instead of annoyed. By practicing more rational self-messages in the group, perhaps students can begin to react in more rational and helpful ways to stressful situations.

Students, teachers, and project counselors who have had experience with classroom meetings and group discussions about feelings have expressed very positive views about them. These group meetings provided a welcomed change of pace if they were not overused. As a result of these meetings, many introverted students were able to participate in class discussions for the first time.

Resources:
School Counseling: Theories and Concepts, by W. Poppen and C. Thompson (Lincoln, Neb.: Professional Educators Publications, 1974).
For Those Who Care: Ways of Relating to Youth, by C. Thompson and W. Poppen (Columbus, Ohio: Merrill, 1972).

Activity: Brainstorming

Level: Grade 3-Adult

Purpose: To develop an ample supply of topics of interest to students and teach the group a technique for solving problems.

Procedure: Present the idea of brainstorming by having students warm up with a divergent-thinking activity such as a discussion on the question "What are the advantages of having trees in one's house yard?" or "What are all possible uses of broken Ping-Pong balls?" During the warm-up introduce the rule of not evaluating any of the ideas until the brainstorming is over.

Members of the class may be divided into groups of five or six. One member may be designated as a recorder and another member may be selected to enforce the rule of no idea evaluation. All ideas are written on a large sheet of paper that should be visible to all members of the group. A five-minute practice session might be held on another warm-up topic such as "What are all the ways in which people might learn if they lived in a world with no books?" After the practice the group can check to see whether all ideas were recorded and criticism avoided.

The actual brainstorming should be done on a specific question — for example, "What topics would interest most of you and lead to a fun discussion?" — and last approximately ten minutes. After the brainstorming, the duplicate ideas on the list can be combined and a master list of discussion topics posted somewhere in the classroom. Any student can add a new idea to the posted list at any time thereafter.

One variation of this idea is to give students magazines and ask them to cut out and paste (on poster board) pictures that relate to discussion topics. The actual topic question should be written under each picture. The resulting posters (each a collage) can be displayed to remind students of the class-meeting topics. Another variation is to ask students to write on a slip of paper a topic they would like to discuss and place it in a "topic box."

The brainstorming technique can also be used during social-problem-solving meetings. The activity of brainstorming is evaluated highly because it is fun and is possibly therapeutic. There are ways of determining whether students have become better problem solvers or idea generators as a result of brainstorming.

Students appreciate the opportunity to make their own choice about topics. Quoting one of the project counselors, "Those classes using the topic box decided that at least one meeting a week should be decided by the surprise method of drawing a topic from the box."

Resource:
Psychology of Problem Solving, by G.A. Davis (New York: Basic Books, 1973).

Activity: Listening Game

Level: Grade 1-Adult

Purpose: To learn that listening is a skill necessary for effective classroom group meetings.

Procedure: During any classroom group discussion on a subject of special interest to the class, interrupt the discussion and tell the students that, before anyone speaks, he or she must summarize what the previous speaker has said. Anyone in the group may challenge the accuracy of the summaries. Observers can be assigned to determine whether the class members are really listening to one another.

The Listening Game can be enacted periodically for five minutes during class meetings. In order to ensure the development of listening skills, the game should probably be used once every five class meetings. After the class meeting, a brief discussion should be held on how the game has affected listening during the meeting.

Most students enjoy this activity. Many are amazed to discover what poor listeners they often are as a result of their being completely absorbed in what they are going to say when the other person stops talking. According to one project counselor, in a class of 35 third-graders 30 said that they could be better listeners. Invoking the rule of summarizing is a good way to maintain listening skills in the group.

Resources:
The Helping Interview, by A. Benjamin (Boston: Houghton Mifflin, 1969, p. 100).
Teacher and Child, by H. Ginott (New York: Macmillan, 1972, p. 262).

Activity: Listening Triads

Level: Grade 4-Adult

Purpose: To teach listening skills.

Procedure: The class is divided into groups of three; a talker, a listener, and an observer make up each group. The talker is asked to tell the listener, for a period of three minutes, what pleases him or her the most. The observer keeps time and, after the three-minute period, rates the listener's listening behaviors on the following scale.

Listening Scale

No ____ Yes ____   The listener looked at the talker and paid attention to what was being said.
No ____ Yes ____   The listener encouraged the talker by nodding his or her head.
No ____ Yes ____   The listener asked good questions.
No ____ Yes ____   The listener didn't talk too much.
No ____ Yes ____   The listener helped the talker tell about the topic.

Next, the roles are switched, and the topic is changed to what displeases the talker the most or to some other topic. Following the three-minute talk period, the listener, in addition to being rated on the scale by the observer, is asked to summarize the thoughts and feelings expressed by the talker. The talker and observer verify the listener's summary.

Participants are sometimes surprised to learn that the best listeners are those who encourage and help the talker tell his or her story by talking themselves and by using nonverbal expressions of attention. The project counselors found the Listening Triads activity useful in teaching listening behavior for group discussions.

Activity: Mystery Box—20 Questions

Level: Grades 2-6

Purpose: To warm up for class meetings and to develop active-listening, thinking, and remembering skills.

Materials: A pencil, paper for keeping score, a box, and different articles to put in the box.

Procedure: Have the children form a circle. Explain that the Mystery Box game involves listening, remembering, and thinking skills, because the goal is to guess the mysterious contents of the box by asking no more than 20 questions. Designate a leader, a name caller, and a scorekeeper. The name caller calls on one of the students whose hand is raised. The student asks the leader a question that will be answered "Yes," or "No," or "I don't know." The scorekeeper keeps a running count of the number of questions asked. If 20 questions have been asked and the mystery is not solved, the leader is the winner. If, instead, the mystery is solved with 20 questions or less, the class is the winner. The student who guesses the mysterious contents can be assigned to present the game at the next meeting. As a variation or as a warm-up, students can play this game with numbers: "I'm thinking of a number between 1 and 1000. What is it?" One class of second-graders came up with the idea of guessing a letter of the alphabet using only ten questions.

Classes seem to enjoy this game immensely. It affords an opportunity for everybody in class to become involved. The children who are having trouble achieving academically have an opportunity for recognition. Everyone wants to be the mystery presenter, the name caller, or the scorekeeper. Any child can learn to play these roles effectively. The roles of name caller and scorekeeper can be used to promote student involvement. "Disruptive" students who are assigned these roles are too busy to misbehave.

Resource:
Teacher and Child, by H. Ginott (New York: Macmillan, 1972, p. 260).

Activity: Class Interview of a Visitor or Group Member

Level: Grade 1-Adult

Purpose: To have students learn how to ask pertinent questions, how to focus on one thing as a group, and how to express themselves before a group while being the center of attention.

Materials: Tape recorder.

Procedure: The counselor or teacher introduces this activity by asking the group the following questions: Have you seen or heard TV or radio programs in which people are interviewed about themselves? What types of questions are they asked? What would you like to know about _____ if he or she were the subject of a TV interview and you were the interviewer? (*Note:* Students may be asked to write out questions before the meeting and bring them to the interview.) One of the students is interviewed by the group. The tape is then available at a listening center so the students, especially the one interviewed, can listen to the interview after the meeting. The activity is extremely valuable if teachers allow themselves to be interviewed. A variation is to have a student role-play an ideal parent, ideal teacher, or ideal student being interviewed. One classroom follows the procedure of highlighting one student each week. The group interview is the focal point of that procedure.

Resource:
Values Clarification, by S. Simon, L. Howe, and H. Kirschenbaum (New York: Hart, 1972).

Activity: Expressing Feelings to the Group

Level: Grades 4-6

Purpose: To increase the students' ability to express feelings, the reasons for these feelings, and expectations of others.

Materials: Filmstrip *What Do You Expect of Others?*

Procedure: The filmstrip makes suggestions that the counselor may elect to follow. Alternate suggestions not in the filmstrip guide are:

1. After viewing, discuss what one expects of a police officer, fire fighter, mother, father, teacher, and so on.
2. Use the statement "I feel _____ when I see _____ because _____ "
   to lead the students into expressing feelings and telling why they feel as they do. Example: I feel *nervous* when I see *a police officer* because *I'm afraid he knows I've done something wrong.*

Students like to put their feelings into words and discover why they feel the way they do in certain situations. Students also learn one way of responding empathically to feelings.

Resource:
What Do You Expect of Others?, a filmstrip by Guidance Associates (757 Third Ave., New York, N.Y. 10017).

Activity: Stop-Stop

Level: Elementary-Adult

Purpose: To explore feelings students have when they are interrupted and to practice making concise statements.

Procedure: The students count off by numbers. Have odd-number students sit on chairs on one side of the room and have even-number students sit on the floor on the other side of the room. Suggest topic for discussion — for example, "Why go to school?" or "How can we help with the energy crisis?" Establish the following rules:

1. Odd-number students can make two statements or suggestions at a time.
2. Even-number students can make only one statement at a time.
3. Odd-number students can say "Stop-Stop" when evens are talking, and evens must stop.

The counselor acts as the referee and keeps the game moving. After ten minutes, change sides and repeat the game.

Students learn how important it is to keep communication brief yet accurate and to avoid interruption.

Activity: The Hat Game

Level: Grade 5-Adult

Purpose: To explore feelings created by reactions of others to oneself and effects of such reactions on one's self-concept.

Materials: Seven strips of paper 3 inches wide and 16 inches long or seven strips of masking tape; seven paper clips.

Procedure: Label each strip with one of the following:

Laugh at what I say.
Ignore me.
Agree with me.
Disagree with me.
Ask me questions.
Turn away from me.
Respect me.

Arrange seven students in a small circle and the remaining students in a larger circle around the smaller group. Assign various observation tasks to the students in the outside circle. Using the paper clips, make hats out of the seven paper strips and place one on the head of each student in the small circle. Each participant can see what the hats say, except the one that he or she is wearing. For best results give the "Ignore me" hat to a popular student. Assign to the small group a controversial topic of interest for discussion. Ask all members to react to one another in the way described by the respective hats and to try to come to an agreement about the topic. Discussion ends when members discover, through the others' reactions, what their own hat says. The participants then look at their hats.

Many questions related to feelings and behavior should follow, some concerning the participants' own feelings — for example, "What happened during the discussion?" and "How did you feel?" — and some concerning the behavior of the other participants — for example, "How did he or she behave when you reacted in the way the hat described?" and "Did he or she continue to contribute to the discussion? If so, why? If not, why?" The discussion may involve all students present, including those who did not participate. The observers may be asked "What did you observe?" and "Did a leader emerge in the group? Who was it and why?" This exercise has proven very effective in developing better relationships among group members and more effective working conditions within groups. It has been especially well received by students in grades 5 through 8.

Activity: What My Appearance Says

Level: Grade 4-Adult

Purpose: To become aware of clothes and of the impression our clothes make on others.

Materials: Pencils and ditto sheets.

Procedure: Give each student a ditto sheet. Tell the students to list in column 1 five items of clothing or jewelry that they are wearing and to write in column 2 what they think each item says about themselves. For example, a red shirt might say "I want to be noticed!"

Instruct the students to fold the paper so that column 2 is hidden and to pass it to the student on their left. This student writes in column 3 what he or she thinks that the five items in column 1 say about the student in question.

Return the paper to the original student (on right) and compare the two columns. Share with the group what you and others think you are trying to say with your clothing. Some students are surprised to find out that clothing can say so much.

Resource:
Values Clarification, by S. Simon, L. Howe, and H. Kirschenbaum (New York: Hart, 1972).

Activity: Exploring Self-Concept

Level: Grades 1-3

Purpose: To help the counselor find out how each student sees himself or herself.

Materials: Modeling clay.

Procedure: Have the students choose the clay of the color they wish to use and ask them to make their own faces with the clay. Allow students enough time to finish (about 15 minutes). Make sure each child who wishes has an opportunity to show his or her work.

This activity leads to a discussion of how we see ourselves, how others see us, and what we think about ourselves. The counselor directs the discussion with questions such as "Who is that?" "Why does Tim's hair look like that?" "How did you know how to make your hair look like that?" "Why are Mike's eyes different from Annie's?" "What do you like about Sylvia?" The children are complimented on their efforts and encouraged to add other features to their models. Children usually want to do the activity again during the next group session.

ACTIVITIES FOR A SELF-CONCEPT LEARNING CENTER

The learning center is a collection of learning activities and experiences designed to stimulate student learning and exploration about self, others, and the environment. The learning center offers students the opportunity to build their sense of self-esteem by achieving success in their independent learning activities.

Most independent learning activities involve self-selection, self-direction, and self-motivation on the students' part. The learning center described herein focuses on self-concept development; however, almost any subject can be taught through the learning-center concept.

The learning center can occupy a space either in the classroom or in the hall. One of the project[1] centers organized it in the hall to provide a broader experience for the children as they shared their learning activities with one another. In fact the students were often involved in the construction of the center. Sections of the center were constructed with tables, chairs, and desks pushed together; others were highlighted with mobiles hanging overhead.

Specific learning objectives are established for each activity, but the students are encouraged to express their creativity. Learning objectives are most helpful when they are clearly stated in language that students can understand. Class meetings are a good way to introduce a new learning center by stimulating the students' curiosity.

The learning center offers the students an opportunity to make their own choices. Many find such opportunity most refreshing, while others prefer to maintain a teacher/student relationship in which the teacher makes all the choices. Therefore, another objective of the learning center is to facilitate student development in the areas of decision making and consideration of choices. Choices are offered in materials, methods, and procedures for achieving objectives. Students may choose from games, worksheets, reading material, and various audiovisual aids available in the centers. Learning activities may be carried out alone, in pairs, or in small groups. Sequential learning activities allow students to work at their own rate and to achieve at the level of their choice.

Individual student contracts are helpful in the management and evaluation process, especially when they are used with a sign-out sheet. The contracts help students develop and follow through on their commitments. A sample contract and sign-out sheet are included on p. 27.

[1]The term *project* refers throughout the book to the Multi-Center Elementary School Guidance Project.

Contract

I agree to complete activities number <u>1, 2, 3, 4, 5, 6, 7, and 8</u>

Signed _____ (Student)

Signed _____ (Teacher)

Sign-Out Sheet

Name	Monday	Tuesday	Wednesday	Thursday	Friday
	1	2,3	4,5	6	7,8

Appointment sheets for arranging an evaluation conference are available to the students. Such evaluations generally consist of a short oral or written performance quiz about the center's learning objectives.

The learning center does take time to construct, but it may be used over a two- or three-week period, depending on the topic and the students. Teachers may choose to add to their learning centers over the years and to swap centers. The learning center is one way of encouraging students to go through the creative process of producing new solutions to problem situations. The most important result of this process is the opportunity for the child to approach a problem from a new perspective.

Activity: Building a Vocabulary of Feeling Words

Purpose: To increase the number of positive and negative feeling words that students use in expressing themselves.

Materials: Two poster boards, construction paper, and glue.

Procedure: Make a "happy sunflower" on one board and a "frowny-face umbrella" on the other one. Petals with positive-feeling words can be added to the happy face to turn it into a warm sunflower, and raindrops with negative-feeling words can be added to the umbrella.

Activity: Relating Feelings to Behaviors

Purpose: To enable students to identify feeling words and to relate these words to behaviors.

Materials: Poster board, construction paper, and glue.

Procedure: Make a puzzle page of pleasant- and unpleasant-feeling words. Ask the students to draw a happy face on pleasant-feeling words and a frowny face on unpleasant-feeling words. They may check with a key to see whether their answers match. Students may draw a picture using one or more of these feeling words, or they may write a story using five of these feeling words.

Activity: Recognizing Expressions of Feelings

Purpose: To help students listen for and identify the feeling words used in a story.

Procedure: Students listen to a story and record the feeling words on paper. They may check their list with the teacher's answer key. Students may make up their own story with the words from a list or with opposite-feeling words.

Activity: Open-Ended Puzzle Stories

Purpose: To encourage students to use their imagination to identify and express feelings and relate them to behaviors.

Materials: Poster board, magazine illustrations, and glue.

Procedure: Choose pictures filled with action and interest. Make puzzles for your students by cutting magazine pictures into pieces. A story without an ending is made up for each puzzle. Students write endings to the stories after they have solved the puzzle.

Activity: Choice Cards

Purpose: To challenge the student's imagination.

Materials: Poster board, magazine illustrations, and glue.

Procedure: Students answer questions such as "Which house would you like to live in?" "Which hat do you want to wear?" and "Which shoe is for you?" selecting from the illustrations mounted on the poster boards. The students are asked to tell why they made a particular choice.

Activity: Relating Feelings to Behavior through Writing

Purpose: To enable students to identify feeling words, to relate them to actions, and to make up original stories, poems, or songs about one of them.

Materials: Poster board, magazine illustrations, and glue.

Procedure: Select pictures filled with action and of interest to the children. Choose pictures that depict feelings. Ask the children to write stories, poems, or songs that incorporate the feelings shown in the pictures. Also ask them to include in their writing what people usually do when they have that particular feeling.

Activity: What Happened Next?

Purpose: To develop the ability to make choices through creative writing.

Materials: Poster board, magazine illustrations, and glue.

Procedure: Display a group of pictures, all related to one story but not arranged in the proper sequence. Cut-up comic strips may be used. Students arrange the pictures in the correct order from left to right and write original stories, poems, or songs about one of the picture sequences.

Activity: What If?

Purpose: To see alternatives in our everyday environment.

Materials: Poster board, magazine illustrations, and glue.

Procedure: Alternatives to everyday things in the students' environment are presented — for example, "What if there were no signs?" Magazine illustrations of signs to which students are exposed every day are prepared.

Students answer questions such as "Would you like it?" "What would happen?" "Would it be good or bad?" and "Why or why not?"

Activity: Story Recipes

Purpose: To increase the students' self-selection, self-direction, and self-motivation.

Materials: Poster board, magazine illustrations, and glue.

Procedure: Present posters with interesting pictures — for example, two witches, a tent, and a jeep. Instruct the students to take a poster and think how all the posters could be used to make stories, poems, or songs. Encourage the students to write or tell what thought or feelings the pictures evoke in them.

Activity: Feelings and Thoughts Collages

Purpose: To develop a positive self-concept.

Materials: Construction paper, old magazines, scissors, and glue.

Procedure: Write several titles on a large sheet of construction paper — for example, "Things That Make Me Feel Happy," "Things I Do Well," "Something That Makes Someone Feel Good," "Something That Makes Someone Feel Bad," and "My Family and Things I Can Do to Help Them." The students cut out from old magazines pictures that express these feelings and thoughts and paste them under the appropriate titles.

Activity: The Mind-Excursion Travel Folder

Purpose: To increase the students' self-selection, self-direction, and self-motivation.

Materials: Poster board, construction paper, glue, and sample travel folder.

Procedure: Students make their own travel folders by copying the example and by following the instructions contained in the model folder.

The instructions are:

1. Choose a name for your imaginary land.
2. Write the name on the cover.
3. Draw yourself in your land.
4. Draw an imaginary animal that lives in your land.
5. What do people in your land like to do?
6. What kind of feelings do people in your land have?
7. Draw something very special about your land.
8. Fold a large piece of poster board into a stand-up model advertising your land.

Resources:

"The Counselor's Workshop: Learning Centers — An Approach to Developmental Guidance," by R. Myrick (*Elementary School Guidance and Counseling*, 1973, *7*, 58-63).

"Creativity: Everybody's Business," by D. Shallcross (*Personnel and Guidance Journal*, 1973, *51*, 623-626).

Individualizing Instruction and Keeping Your Sanity, by W. Bechtol (Chicago: Follett, 1973).

For Those Who Care: Ways of Relating to Youth, by C. Thompson and W. Poppen (Columbus, Ohio: Merrill, 1972).

Chapter Three

DEVELOPING POSITIVE SELF-CONCEPT BY FOCUSING ON STRENGTHS

Effective teachers and counselors focus on the student's strengths, not on the student's weaknesses. They see themselves as developmental educators rather than as remedial helpers; thus, they build on strengths instead of dwelling on inadequacies. Students with low self-opinion are already overly aware of their weaknesses and failures. They suffer very much from the "I'm not OK" syndrome. These students, constantly reminded of their "not OKness" by peers, parents, and teachers, may come to believe that they are destined for failure no matter what they do. Therefore, a very important goal of the school guidance program is to develop positive self-concepts in the students by focusing on strengths.

GROUP ACTIVITIES FOR DEVELOPING POSITIVE SELF-CONCEPT

Activity: Group Strengths Test

Level: Grade 4-Adult

Purpose: To build self-concept through identification of personal strengths by group members.

Materials: Gummed labels, 4 x 6 cards, and pencils.

Procedure: Divide the participants into groups of six and have each group form a circle. Make sure that the circles are arranged so that each student can see all the other students' faces. Generally the circle works better if the participants are seated close together. Next, ask each student in turn to tell the group a few things about himself or herself by discussing the following "sharing topics":

1. What are three adjectives that describe you and why?
2. What is the best thing you have accomplished and why?
3. What is your favorite activity and why?
4. What is something you are looking forward to in the next few days and why?
5. Who is one person who has a strong influence on your life and why?

Depending on the time available, you may choose to have the group go around on two or more of the above topics. In fact, you may want to add other topics for discussion. The information-sharing process has two purposes: fostering a sense of openness and empathy among the group members and developing a basis for looking at the individual strengths of the group members.

After the discussion of the "sharing topics," give each participant a gummed label for each member of his or her group (for example, in a group of six each member receives five labels). Ask the students to write on each of the five labels the name of one individual in the group and all the strengths and good points they observed in that individual. When this phase of the exercise is completed, each group member will have a label and a list of strengths for each of his or her fellow group members. All the participants are then given a blank 4 x 6 card and are instructed to focus on one member of the group as he or she passes his or her card around the circle. As the card is passed to a fellow group member, the member sticks the appropriate label on the card and tells the "passer" what strengths are listed on the label and why. Ask the group members to be as specific as possible in describing these strengths. General comments such as "You are a good guy" are less helpful than "I like the way you express your opinions."

After all the members have been in the spotlight and have received their five strength labels (negative comments or criticisms are not permitted), ask them to think of a goal they would like to meet or a task they need to complete. Preferably this goal or task should be something that can be completed in the next seven to ten days. Then ask the participants to share with the group the nature of the task they have chosen and to select a "commitment partner." The "commitment partner" has the task to call on the group member at an agreed time to see whether the task has been completed. Students are encouraged to use their lists of strengths to complete their tasks. In fact, interesting discussions often center on each member's favorite strength description by the group. You may also want to ask your students to tell how they feel about their strengths cards after they have received feedback from each group member. If building commitment is one of your major interests as a counselor, you may want to ask each student to post his or her commitment on the wall and then to check back with the group when the commitment has been met.

Activity: The Compliment Game

Level: Grade K-Adult (with modifications, the game can be adapted to any age group)

Purpose: To develop the ability to focus on one another's strengths and to become reinforcing people. Reinforcing people are popular and successful because others like to be around them. This activity can also be helpful to teachers and parents.

Procedure: This activity, too, works better when the group is divided into smaller groups of, say, six people. The group interaction may be started by having the members talk briefly about one thing of which they are proud — a personal characteristic or something they do well. Then the members are asked to talk about their most successful experiences and why they consider such experiences more successful than others. Differences in personal values are quite noticeable in this phase of the discussion.

Following the sharing of personal information, preferences, and values, ask the participants to go around the group and pay each member a compliment based on the information that has been exchanged and on other available data. You may wish to have each member in turn pay the person on his or her left a compliment; then reverse the order and have each member in turn pay the person on his or her right a compliment.

When this phase is completed, ask the group members to tell how it feels to give and to receive compliments. Two additional questions may be considered by the group: "Who are the people who compliment you now?" and "On what occasions do you need someone to compliment you?"

A technique used in transactional analysis may be applied to this activity. In transactional analysis, compliments and criticisms are referred to as *positive strokes* and *negative strokes*, respectively. Sometimes we give conditional positive strokes — for example, when we say things such as "I love you because you are always polite." Unconditional positive strokes are generally more valued because there are no strings attached to the message "I love you." Examples of conditional and unconditional negative strokes are "I don't like you when you hit others" and "I just don't like you."

After describing the differences among the four types of strokes, ask the students to go around the group and practice each of the four strokes with the person sitting on their left or right. It should be kept in mind that the negative strokes are just as important as the positive ones in helping people become more aware of how they affect others. With young children the terms *warm fuzzies* and *cold pricklies* are substituted for positive and negative strokes and the terms *conditional* and *unconditional* are omitted.

Activity: The Strengths-Trade Game

Level: Grade 4-Adult (this game has often been used by the project counselors in their in-service training work with teachers and parent-education groups)

Purpose: To help the participants improve their self-image. The activity is based on the theory that we all need something positive on which to build when we want to improve our self-image. We often harbor so many negative feelings about ourselves for so long that we become incapable of seeing the good things about ourselves. Generally people with a poor concept of themselves are very surprised to learn that others see positive things in them. The Strengths-Trade Game helps people to realize what their positive qualities are and to practice positive thinking about themselves and others. In other words, this activity helps people to move toward the "I'm OK—You're OK" view. Another benefit of this game is that it affords the participants the opportunity to compare their self-images with the images others hold of them. One index of our mental adjustment may be the degree of agreement between how we view ourselves and how others view us.

Procedure: Participants are given a list with the names of all group members, including their own, and are asked to write the following two things about each person (except themselves):

1. His or her most outstanding positive physical characteristic (for example: shiny hair, well dressed, nice eyes, good posture, strong body, well coordinated).
2. His or her most outstanding positive personality characteristic (for example: warm, polite, courteous, friendly, conscientious, interesting, fun, humorous, witty, energetic, hard working, helpful, good leader).

After this has been done, ask the group members to write the following two things about themselves:

1. Their three most positive physical features, ranking them as they think others would rank them.
2. Their three most positive personality features, ranking them as they think others would rank them.

The group leader collects all the papers and reads the positive features for each person. These features are then compared with those that the person wrote for himself or herself. The winner is the member who guesses what his or her most positive characteristics are as seen by others. In this game, however, everyone is the winner. Positive thinking about self and others ("I'm OK—You're OK") is a main theme in a winner's script.

The Strengths-Trade Game

Characteristics of others:

Name of group member	Outstanding positive physical characteristic	Outstanding positive personality characteristic
_____	_____	_____
_____	_____	_____
_____	_____	_____
_____	_____	_____

Your own characteristics:

Your name	Outstanding positive physical characteristics	Outstanding positive personality characteristics
_____	1. _____	1. _____
	2. _____	2. _____
	3. _____	3. _____

Activity: Strengths Listing

Level: Grade 3-Adult

Purpose: To help students improve their opinion of themselves by becoming aware of the strengths others see in them; to help students use their strengths to overcome blocks to personal development that others have noticed in them.

Procedure: Participants are asked to interview four important people in their lives and ask them "What do you see as my strengths or strong points?" Younger children may limit their interviews to one or both parents. The person being interviewed is requested to be as specific as possible in compiling the list of strengths. For example:

1. You have a neat appearance.
2. You are a good athlete.
3. You do well in reading.
4. You are friendly.
5. You have a nice smile.
6. You play the piano well.

Following the listing of these strengths, the person being interviewed is asked to mention one thing that the student needs to work on or improve. The student may have a real block to personal development that needs to be removed. For example:

1. I wish you would be on time when I am supposed to meet you.
2. You would probably be better off if you didn't put things off until the last minute.
3. Your fights with Tom don't seem to help you.
4. I wish you would do those things you promise to do.

The activity seems to work best when only one block is mentioned and only after all the strengths have been listed. The block should be something that the student can change if he or she so wishes. One desired outcome is the recognition by the student that he or she has many strengths from which to draw in removing blocks to personal growth and development. A frequent and important by-product of this activity is an improvement in the relationship between the student and the persons being interviewed (parents, teachers, peers, siblings, neighbors, and even bosses). In fact, the Strengths Listing exercise doubles in value when the listings are reciprocal; that is, the student writes down a list of strengths for the person being interviewed. Two helpful ways to end the exercise are to add one more strength to the list after discussing the block and to discuss plans for working on overcoming the block.

Activity: Strengths Badge

Level: Grades K-6

Purpose: To increase feelings of self-esteem by focusing on what one does well.

Materials: Colorful paper, crayons, scissors, and safety pins.

Procedure: The students make a drawing depicting something they do well. Then they make badges out of their drawings and wear the badges the rest of the day. The badge works best when the student writes "I am good at _____" and lets the drawing explain the rest.

The badges can represent the springboard for a classroom discussion on "Things I do well." As a follow-up activity students can construct "I'm a Winner!" badges to wear and to hang up at home. In fact, the Strengths Badge activity could be adapted to feeling classes and to values-clarification activities (see below). Students can wear badges or buttons describing their feelings or positions on various value issues being considered by the class. For example, if the class is discussing whether people should be required to wear seat belts in cars, students may wear badges indicating their position about this issue.

Students receive individual help from the resources available in guidance offices.

Activity: Values-Clarification Exercise

Level: Grade K-Adult

Purpose: To help students realize the difference between respecting another's opinion and agreeing or disagreeing with it. To help students feel good about themselves in spite of the fact that their values may differ from those of the majority ("I'm OK and you're OK even if we disagree"). To foster a good classroom environment by allowing discussion time for topics that call for opinions rather than absolute answers or memorized data.

Procedure: The counselor or teacher may introduce the exercise by printing out the three purposes listed above. It is usually helpful to mention that there are no wrong answers to questions concerning value positions. For example, a favorite group activity centers around a "values continuum," on which the students are asked to sign their name (or initials) to graphically indicate their position on a particular issue. The continuum is drawn on the board, and the middle-ground (no opinion) area is blocked out (see Figure 3-1). The counselor or teacher may explain to the group that the middle area of the continuum is for noncommitters or "compulsive moderates" who have not examined their position on many issues. The extremes of the continuum are represented on the board by the two most extreme views on the issue. Figure 3-1 illustrates how the values continuum would look if the class were examining the issue of awarding or not awarding letter grades to students.

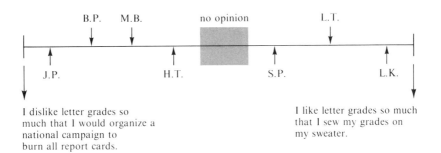

Figure 3-1. Values continuum.

After each student has had the opportunity to sign in, another continuum is drawn, and the students are asked to check the spot on the line that indicates how hard they work for letter grades. Thus, the two continuums offer students the opportunity to see the difference between what they state as a value and what they actually do about it. Discussion following each sign-in period may focus on why the students chose a certain position and why there are discrepancies between value positions and behaviors. Such discrepancies can be quite wide in the areas of smoking, drinking, drug abuse, cheating, shoplifting, dropping out of school, and sex.

As is the case with any group discussion, the participants, including the leader, have the right to pass on any portion of the exercise or discussion. Also, good discussion leaders would not ask questions or deal with issues that they would not answer or tackle themselves.

Activity: Values Auction

Level: Grade 1-Adult (if modified to fit the vocabulary and interest levels of younger children or young adults)

Purpose: To help students examine their values and priorities in life.

Procedure: Each participant is given an imaginary sum of money or a certain amount of play money with which to bid on the items for sale in the auction. Participants will need to budget their money in order to successfully bid on the items they like most. An auctioneer is appointed to sell the first four or five items, and then someone else is given a chance to be auctioneer. Auctioneers can join in on the bidding. One participant is appointed as a clerk to record all sales and the amount of money each participant has spent. The clerk, too, can bid on the items for sale. The number of items to be included in the bill of sale depends on the attention span of the class members. A sample bill of sale with 34 items is included as a guide to the counselor or teacher. Figuring two or three minutes per item, an auction using all 34 items would probably last a little over an hour. Also included is a list of 17 values, each of which identifies two items on the bill of sale. Of course, the counselor or teacher is encouraged to write his or her own bill of sale to explore other values or provide a more intense exploration of the values included.

Following the auction, the counselor or teacher may lead a discussion on the values that seem to be most important to each individual and to the group in general. A most useful procedure is to follow up the discussion period by asking the group to check off those items they want to obtain someday. Frequently children and adults are surprised by the number of possibilities they become aware of through the bill of sale.

Once again, value-clarification discussions and activities provide a good atmosphere for developing a healthy self-concept. All answers are right for the person giving them. Therefore, no failure is possible during this part of the school day. Students also become aware of the worth they ascribe to various objects, behaviors, and practices in their environment. From these value-clarifying experiences students develop the value systems that regulate their behavior—both consciously and unconsciously.

Values Auction

Bill of Sale

Items to be auctioned	Amount budgeted	Highest amount bid	Won by
1. A chance to make everybody treat others fairly			
2. Enough money to help all the sick and poor people in the world			
3. A chance to become a famous person (movie star, baseball player, and so on)			
4. All "A"s on your grade cards			
5. One year of doing your favorite thing as much as you want			
6. A chance to know the answer to an important question			
7. A secret pill that makes people tell the truth			
8. A chance to make your own school assignments			
9. A chance to be the richest person in the world			
10. A chance to be the President of the United States			
11. A friend you can call your very best friend			
12. A house in the most beautiful place in the world			
13. A chance to be the most attractive person in the world			
14. A chance to live to 100 with no illness			

Items to be auctioned	Amount budgeted	Highest amount bid	Won by
15. Someone who will help you with your problems	_____	_____	_____
16. A complete library of your favorite books	_____	_____	_____
17. A talk with any head of state in the world	_____	_____	_____
18. A chance to make all people treat others the way they want others to treat them	_____	_____	_____
19. A chance to give a million dollars to people who need money	_____	_____	_____
20. Being voted Outstanding Person in the class	_____	_____	_____
21. A chance to be the best student in the subject of your choice	_____	_____	_____
22. A year with nothing to do but enjoy yourself	_____	_____	_____
23. A chance to be the wisest person in the world and to make only right decisions for one year	_____	_____	_____
24. A special device that makes people honest	_____	_____	_____
25. A chance to be your own boss	_____	_____	_____
26. A room full of pennies	_____	_____	_____
27. A chance to boss 500,000 people	_____	_____	_____

Items to be auctioned	Amount budgeted	Highest amount bid	Won by
28. Being liked by everyone in the class	_____	_____	_____
29. Tickets to attend any concert, play, opera, or ballet for one year anywhere in the world	_____	_____	_____
30. A hairstyle of your choice and all new clothes	_____	_____	_____
31. Membership in a great health and body-building club	_____	_____	_____
32. A pill for solving problems that make you worry	_____	_____	_____
33. Your own computer for any and all answers you might need	_____	_____	_____
34. A chance to spend six months with any person you have heard about in church or read about in the Bible	_____	_____	_____

Values-Auction Key

Values	Items	Values	Items
Justice	1, 18	Power	10, 27
Service	2, 19	Love	11, 28
Recognition	3, 20	Aesthetics	12, 29
Achievement	4, 21	Physical appearance	13, 30
Pleasure	5, 22	Health	14, 31
Wisdom	6, 23	Emotional well-being	15, 32
Honesty	7, 24	Knowledge	16, 33
Autonomy	8, 25	Religion or morality	17, 34
Wealth	9, 26		

Activity: Self-Concept Topics for Classroom Meetings

Level: Grades K-Adult

Purpose: To foster healthy self-concept development through successful participation in a group; to create a feeling of belonging in all group members; to facilitate further examination of personal strengths and abilities.

Procedure: The following topics are listed as suggestions to counselors and teachers who wish to add variety to classroom meetings focusing on self-concept development.

Distribute some printed incomplete sentences and ask the participants to complete them. If the participants are too young to read and write, the activity may be done orally. Here are some typical examples of incomplete sentences:

1. Last year I couldn't _____.
2. This year I can _____.
3. I used to be a _____.
4. Now I am a _____.
5. If I were a car, I'd like to be a _____.
6. One think I would like to change about myself is _____.
7. I am good at _____.
8. A good friend is _____.
9. I am afraid to _____.

Each of these topics can be used as a subject for discussion. Frequently the group leader can use two topics together — for example, "Last year I couldn't _____, and this year I can _____." The discussion is facilitated by inviting the group members to talk more about their answers. For example, the question concerning which car the participants would like to be may be followed by detailed descriptions of the chosen car's features — color, condition, performance record, and repair record.

Role playing can be incorporated into this activity. For example, the topic "I'm afraid to _____" can be role-played by group members by focusing on how to handle the fear or how to overcome the type of anxiety that prevents one from doing his or her best work.

Another modification is to have the students draw or sketch the objects of their fear and then have the group share and discuss these drawings. A favorite medium for sketching and sharing is the Coat of Arms activity. Each student is given a drawing of a shield divided into six sections (see Figure 3-2). The students fill each section with a drawing that describes

COAT OF ARMS

Without concern for artistic results, fill in
the six areas of the drawing below to make your
own personal coat of arms.

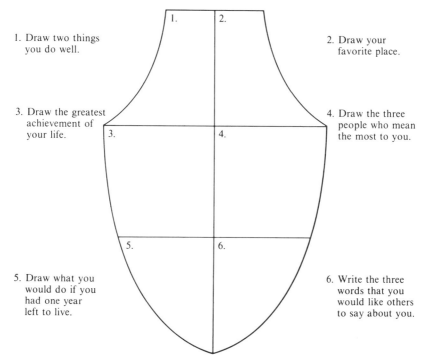

1. Draw two things
   you do well.

2. Draw your
   favorite place.

3. Draw the greatest
   achievement of
   your life.

4. Draw the three
   people who mean
   the most to you.

5. Draw what you
   would do if you
   had one year
   left to live.

6. Write the three
   words that you
   would like others
   to say about you.

Figure 3-2. Coat of arms. (From *Values Clarification: A Handbook of Strategies for Teachers and Students,* by Sidney B. Simon, Leland W. Howe, and Howard Kirschenbaum. Copyright 1972 by Hart Publishing Company, Inc.)

or illustrates something about them. The following are frequently used subjects for the drawings:

1. Two things I love to do
2. The three people who mean the most to me
3. My greatest achievement
4. Something I value or my favorite thing
5. Three words that describe me
6. The school subject I am best at
7. My favorite song or music
8. My favorite book
9. Something or somebody important in my life

Activity: Writing an Ad for Yourself

Level: Grade 1-Adult

Purpose: To focus on individual strengths, skills, and talents as a means of improving poor self-concept.

Materials: Art materials and old magazines.

Procedure: You may start a group discussion by asking the participants what makes a good advertisement. (For example, good ads catch your attention, tell you things you want to know, and convince you to buy the product or service being advertised.)

Then ask the group members to write an ad about themselves that "sells" their strong points and best qualities to others. Art materials and old magazines may be used to make the ads more attractive. A helpful hint to students is to make a list of all their skills, abilities, experiences, and so forth before starting the ad. In fact, the personal strengths identified in the other strengths exercises contained in this book can be used to prepare the ads.

When the group members have completed their ads, they are given some time to share their ads with the other participants. Many people, especially older students and adults, find it difficult to talk about their strengths. For these people the group discussion and sharing of strengths become procedures for building self-confidence.

Children in the primary grades can be assisted in writing ads that are in line with their ability to read and write. Because of their exposure to television, many students are already experts on television commercials. They can therefore adapt these commercials to their own personal ads. Here is one such adaptation:

> Did you know that Jimmy B. caught ten fish last Saturday?
> I didn't know that!
> Did you know that Jimmy B. has never missed a day of school this year?
> I didn't know that!
> Did you know that Jimmy B. has read 17 library books this year?
> I didn't know that!

Activity: What Is Your Bag?

Level: Grade K-Adult

Purpose: This activity offers group members the opportunity to present themselves to the group. In a sense the activity builds on the share-and-tell activities that many teachers already use. When students or group members take turns talking about themselves to the group, they develop confidence in their ability to speak to a group of people. They also have an opportunity to compare their interests, values, and self-concepts with those of their fellow group members.

Procedure: The participants are asked to bring a bag that they have decorated and filled with items that tell something about themselves. Younger students may be asked to bring three things in their bags to share with the group. Older students may be asked to decorate the outside of their bags in ways that reflect how most people see them and the inside of the bag in ways that reflect how they think they really are. In other words, the outside of the bag represents the image the student presents to the outside world, and the inside of the bag represents the image the student has of himself or herself.

How much of the bag the students want to share with the rest of the class or group is a decision they are asked to make for themselves. The activity works best if a time limit is used for each presentation. The time limit could vary from one minute for younger students to five minutes for older students. Also helpful is to ask the students to explain why something in or on the bag is meaningful to them.

A follow-up activity is to have the students write a descriptive sentence or two about themselves. The teacher or counselor collects these statements, reads them to the group, and asks the group to guess who wrote what and why. Both the What Is Your Bag? activity and its Guess Who variation help students examine how they see themselves versus how others see them. One of the activity's subgoals is to help students put these two perspectives together in order to develop a consistent positive view of themselves.

TEACHER/PARENT ACTIVITIES FOR DEVELOPING POSITIVE SELF-CONCEPT IN CHILDREN

Frequently the counselors involved in the Multi-Center Elementary Guidance Project were called upon to conduct in-service education programs for both teachers and parents on how to foster positive self-concept in their students and children. Being teachers and parents themselves, the project counselors were well aware of the drudgery of boring, unproductive in-service education meetings. Therefore, it was decided that their programs would be conducted within the framework of the personal-involvement activities being used with the students in the project centers. It was agreed that the parents would be involved in active learning situations rather than in lecture presentations. The underlying philosophy of the total guidance project was that the best learning occurs by doing rather than by merely listening. The counselors attempted to incorporate three phases of learning into their guidance activities with children, parents, and teachers:

1. The tell-me phase
2. The show-me phase
3. The let-me-do-it phase

The best learning occurs when all three phases of the learning process are utilized. When learning does not happen or when it is blocked, generally one or more of the above three phases of learning have broken down.

A further consideration for the parents' and teachers' in-service programs was the need to develop empathy in the adults for the child's situation — especially for the child with a low concept of self. The ways in which teacher and parent behaviors affect the child's self-concept were also examined. The following activities represent an attempt to incorporate the principles of learning mentioned above into workable and helpful sessions for the participants.

Activity: IALAC

Level: Teachers, parents, and children

Purpose: To create an awareness of how negative, critical, and punitive statements affect another's concept of self. One of the best ways to focus on self-concept is to examine what destroys a person's positive self-image.

Procedure: Conduct a short public interview with a volunteer from the group on his or her strengths and friendships. After the interview tell the volunteer "It seems to me that you are quite likable and capable." If the volunteer agrees, he or she receives a sign with the letters IALAC (I Am Likable And Capable) written on it. The entire group may want to become involved in this part of the discussion by telling how they have achieved or have not achieved this IALAC feeling.

Next all the group members receive cards with typical everyday ego-puncturing messages written on them. In transactional-analysis language, these would be called "critical-parent messages." Here are some examples:

"Hey, lazy, get up or you'll be late as usual!"

"Clean up your plate. Don't you know how much it costs to feed you?"

"Don't forget your lunch money. Won't you ever grow up and learn to watch out for yourself?"

"I see you didn't finish your homework again. What do you think happens to irresponsible people like you?"

"You spilled your juice again. You are just clumsy. You always were and you'll always be a klutz."

"Mary Lou, you are the only one in this class who can't understand how to borrow when you subtract. I don't know what to do with you!"

"Why can't you do as well as your sister did when she was in my class?"

"I don't believe you'll ever be able to understand math!"

"Big people don't cry."

"If you paid attention in here, you wouldn't have to move your lips when you read to yourself."

The group is asked to read aloud these messages, directing them to the IALAC volunteer. For each message, depending on how it affects him or her, the volunteer tears off a piece of the IALAC sign. The rougher the comment, the bigger the piece that is torn off — representing the degree of self-concept destroyed. The group members are invited to use their own "favorite" put-down message against the volunteer. The activity continues until the IALAC sign is completely destroyed. Usually a lively discussion follows the demonstration. The group may want to consider other put-down messages and alternative ways to interact with their children and students. A very useful topic of discussion is how to set limits and still maintain a good relationship with one's own students or children. The end point of such a discussion should be how one can say to a child "I love you, but I hate what you are doing!"

Activity: Happygram

Level: Teachers

Purpose: To encourage children by encouraging their parents. Problem situations are generally the only reason why many teachers get in touch with the students' parents. The Happygram procedure works in the opposite way: parents are informed about their children's accomplishments! The project counselors found that the use of Happygrams was one of the most powerful things they could do to improve their students' self-concept.

Procedure: The project counselors made Happygrams out of bright-yellow paper and designed them to look like telegrams. The word *Happygram* was printed across the top of the sheet, with a smiling face in the top right-hand corner (see Figure 3-3).

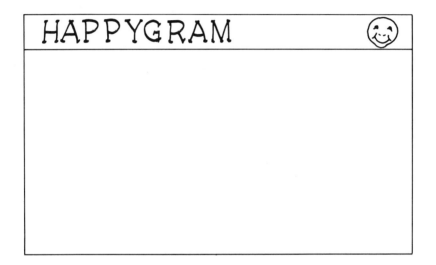

Figure 3-3. Happygram blank.

The message, addressed to parents, described something their child had accomplished — a good grade, better behavior, helpfulness in the classroom, or special awards. The messages were mailed or sealed and sent to parents via their children.

The effect the Happygrams had on the children was amazing. The parents were pleased and passed their feelings on to their children.

Some teachers in the project modified the Happygram activity by making three phone calls per week to parents about something positive their child had done. In many instances the phone calls seemed to get even better results than Happygrams. Of course, it is important to include all the parents of all the children in these activities.

Activity: Leading Class Meetings: The Drug-Abuse Discussion

Level: Teachers and principals

Purpose: One goal of the project is to involve teachers in leading their own classroom meetings. To introduce the concept, the counselor leads a sample classroom meeting with the teachers on drug abuse and self-worth.

Procedure: Distribute a one-page paper or a newspaper article on the topic of drug abuse and ask the participants to read it to themselves. Ask the group how many of them know of any evidence that supports or refutes the article. Also ask the participants whether they have had any personal experience with students or friends who have turned to drugs to escape reality or to mitigate the pain of feeling alone or worthless.

The following example topic sheet, written by Jacqueline Boehler, one of the project counselors, is included for the reader's use as a possible discussion stimulus.

Self-Worth and Drug Abuse

Lack of self-esteem is the one factor that characterizes those adolescents who are dropouts, runaways, drug abusers, and the like. Troubled children don't feel their worth.

Such children hate to try new things because they expect to fail. They talk little and have difficulty expressing their feelings. Their idea of the future is vague and defeatist. They often turn to drugs as an escape. They may be held to their parents by intense psychological ties that interfere with the development of their independence. Encouragement and interest on the part of counselors and teachers can help strengthen these children's feelings of self-worth.

By contrast, normal youngsters are competent and will face challenges even at the risk of failure. They are more verbal and able to express feelings and ideas with more ease. They can visualize the future, which they expect to be interesting and successful. The relationship such students have with their parents enables them to develop independence and a positive self-image.

Dr. Gene M. Smith, a Massachusetts General Hospital psychologist, conducted a study of more than 2000 Boston-area students. He discovered that those who rebel against parents and teachers are more likely to use drugs by the time they reach high school than are more conventional youngsters. Rebels tend to smoke cigarettes early. They make poor grades and tend to score low on such personality traits as conscientiousness, dependability, planning, thoroughness, efficiency, persistency, and ambition. They use alcohol as well as drugs. Heavy marijuana users often are heavy drinkers, too.

Obedient and ambitious students who make good grades are the least likely to turn to drugs or alcohol. Dr. Smith says that in their self-reports these students tend to say "I enjoy being good at things I have to do at school" and "When I am told to do something by a teacher, I do it."

Another study, sponsored by the Mental Health Institute, was conducted by Dr. Norman Z. Brill and Joel Hochman. They found that the younger the students are when they begin to use marijuana, the more likely they are to become heavy users and to continue use after college. Brill and Hochman found that heavy users of marijuana have greater difficulty than moderate users or nonusers in determining and pursuing short- and long-range goals.

Drug-Awareness Inventory

Write "T" by the statements that are true and "F" by the statements that are false. (15 points)

_____ 1. All drugs are dangerous.

_____ 2. Most drugs can have good and bad uses.

_____ 3. Prescription drugs cannot hurt you.

_____ 4. If I misuse drugs, it will kill me.

_____ 5. My parents have told me about drugs.

_____ 6. I know how to react if someone tries to make me take drugs.

_____ 7. It is alright to take a friend's medicine.

_____ 8. Only "bad" people are drug users.

_____ 9. There is nothing I can do for someone who takes drugs.

_____ 10. Learning about drugs is not important.

List three reasons why people may choose to misuse drugs.

_____

_____

_____

List two ways in which a drug user may be helped.

_____

_____

RATIONALE FOR FOSTERING POSITIVE SELF-CONCEPT IN STUDENTS

This book's focus on positive self-concept applies to all areas of emphasis in the elementary and secondary school guidance programs. This is especially true for the area of academic achievement (see Chapter Six), which is crucial to the students' feelings about themselves. Aware of the importance of academic achievement, effective counselors, teachers, and principals work toward creating an educational environment that replaces failure with success and allows each student to experience at least one success per school day. Praise and encouragement are the essential ingredients of this approach.

Second chances to be successful are available in good schools. For example, teachers may give credit even for words that are misspelled. Such credit is fractional, and the amount depends on the ratio between correct and incorrect letters in the word. Credit is given only if the student corrects the mistake and computes the fractional credit correctly. The misspelled word *separete*, for instance, would receive 7/8 of a point (8 letters, 1 mistake). Such fractions of a point would then be added to the other points the student has earned on the test. If some of you believe that by doing so we are teaching bad spelling habits, we invite you to consider the merits of providing a mediational step that encourages the student to make the big jump from failure to success. And don't forget the learning that results from the practical application of fractions!

Instruments 1, 2, 3, and 4 in Appendix C were utilized by the project counselors and teachers to evaluate changes in self-concept for those students who had been found to have low self-concept at the beginning of the school year. Although differences between pretest and posttest scores were tabulated only for the students so identified, the opportunity to participate in the self-concept activities was available to all students.

Chapter Four

PEER
RELATIONSHIPS

Fostering good peer relationships is another objective of school guidance programs. As counselors and teachers are well aware, conflict with peers is one of the five main causes of the problems experienced by their students. These causes are:

1. Conflict with others
2. Conflict with self
3. Lack of skill
4. Lack of information about self
5. Lack of information about the environment

Only by improving relationships among students can the first problem be solved. Of course, the peer-relationship part of the guidance program is open to all students, not just to those experiencing problems with other students. The many group and individual approaches utilized in the peer-relationship part of the guidance program also contribute to the improvement of the students' self-concept. Few things are so vital to our self-esteem as loving and being loved.

The following activities and methods were designed as procedures for improving peer relationships. The activities involve both group and individual approaches with the students. The main emphasis, however, is on group guidance and group-counseling experiences. Instruments 3, 4, and 9 in Appendix C are used to evaluate changes in peer relationships in those students who have been found to have difficulties in getting along with others.

Activity: Active Listening in the Counseling Process

Level: Grade K-Adult

Purpose: To practice active listening. In addition to the reality-therapy and rational-emotive approaches to counseling discussed in Chapter Two, a third approach, based on active listening, is especially appropriate in situations involving peer relationships. According to Rogers' (1951) client-centered approach to counseling, the purpose of active listening is to let clients know that the counselor has heard their message and the feelings associated with the message.

Procedure: Carkhuff (1973) has classified the responses that counselors make to students during the counseling interview into the following five levels.

> *Sam:* Frank is always trying to pick a fight with me, and I don't know how to make him stop it.

Level-1 response:

> *Counselor:* Don't worry about it. I knew a kid like Frank once, and he never amounted to anything.

The level-1 response misses Sam's message, as well as the feelings that the message conveys.

Level-2 response:

> *Counselor:* Maybe you should carry a ball bat with you.

The level-2 response offers Sam a solution before giving him an opportunity to tell his complete story or suggest his own ideas for solving the problem.

Level-3 response:

> *Counselor:* You're feeling annoyed and angry with Frank because he always tries to start trouble with you.

The level-3 response reflects the message and feelings Sam is experiencing at the moment.

Level-4 response:

> *Counselor:* You're feeling annoyed and angry with Frank because he always tries to start trouble with you and you'd like to know how you can make him stop this behavior.

The level-4 response accurately reflects Sam's message and feelings of the moment, but it also echoes Sam's desire to change things.

Level-5 response:

> *Counselor:* Sam, would you like to try solving this difficulty by thinking of something you can do to help solve the problems you have with Frank?

The level-5 response comes after the student has had the opportunity to tell his story. It helps the student develop a plan for moving from where he is to where he would like to be.

Responses at levels 1 and 2 are considered harmful to the counseling process. Responses at level 3 are considered break-even types of responses, which don't especially move or block the counseling process. Responses at levels 4 and 5 are considered helpful because they help students move from where they are to where they would like to be. The process of identifying where one is in relation to where one would like to be is quite helpful in itself if someone wants to change his or her behavior. The counselor may practice level-4 responses by filling in a blank similar to the following one with statements that reflect how the student is feeling, why he or she is feeling that way, and what he or she would like to have happen.

You are feeling _____ because _____, and you want _____.

Activity: Becoming a Reinforcing Person

Level: Grade K-Adult

Purpose: To teach the three basic behaviors involved in becoming a reinforcing person: observing, waiting, and reinforcing. Unfortunately many of us are taught at a very young age not to look at others. We are told not to stare. Staring is impolite! Therefore, many of us never learn a very necessary behavior for becoming reinforcing persons—observing what others are doing.

A lack of the second behavior, waiting, sometimes becomes another block to being a reinforcing person. Punishment and negative reinforcement get quick results and therefore appeal to those people who don't have the patience and wisdom to wait until others do something worthy of an honest compliment. But, while punishment generally does get quick results, the results are often temporary and the relationship between two people is harmed.

The third behavior, giving positive reinforcement, is frequently another skill students and adults need to learn. Some people never reinforce or compliment others, and many who do are either inconsistent with it or do it at the wrong time. Phony compliments and dishonest positive reinforcement don't fool most students. Therefore, it is important that we teach students how to become genuinely reinforcing persons.

Procedure: The class is divided into groups of six. In each of these smaller groups one person volunteers to be the subject and another the experimenter. The experimenter's task is to guide the blindfolded subject to a 5 x 7 card taped to the wall. Whenever the subject makes a move in the right direction, the experimenter reinforces him or her by saying "Warm." The demonstration works best when the subjects extend their right or left arm in front of them and point their hand toward the spot where they think the card is located.

The experimenter is not supposed to use any punishment or any words other than the word *warm*. Each person in the group should have the opportunity to play both roles. It should be explained to the students that a successful experimenter needs to practice the three key behaviors of observing, waiting, and reinforcing. The students should also understand that these three behaviors are necessary not just to be successful experimenters but also to be successful friends, co-workers, customers, bosses, students, employees, patients, clients, and so on. In fact, most people enjoy doing things for reinforcing persons because reinforcing persons make them feel appreciated and worthwhile.

Activity: Ignoring Game

Level: Grades 1-5

Purpose: To make the children aware that the best way to deal with attention-seeking mischievous behavior is to ignore it.

Procedure: Have children form a circle. Tell them that they are going to try a new game called the Ignoring Game. They are to pretend that they are doing a lesson such as spelling or math. One of the children plays the role of the leader and tries to distract the others by talking to them, untying their shoes, writing notes, dropping something, and so forth. Any student who looks up, smiles, or pays attention in other ways is out of the game. The winners are those students who succeed in truly ignoring the annoying attention-seeking behaviors of the leader. The winners then become the leaders.

After the game is over, ask questions about the game. What is ignoring? What happens if one pays attention to mischievous behavior? What would be a better way to be noticed? How could the Ignoring Game be used in class?

Students enjoy the Ignoring Game. Younger children may have some difficulty conceptualizing and effectively coping with the idea that attention-seeking behaviors can be ignored. It is most helpful if the teacher gives positive reinforcement to pupils actually using this game in their everyday life.

Activity: The Four Goals of Misbehavior

Level: Grade 5-Adult

Purpose: To help students become aware of what they are trying to achieve with their misbehaviors and to help them find more helpful ways of securing a place in their family and in their peer group.

Procedure: Discuss with the students why we misbehave and what we are trying to accomplish with our misbehaviors. Usually we misbehave when we are trying to find our place in our family, in our class, or in any other group.

According to Dreikurs (1968), the four goals of misbehavior are:

Attention
Power
Revenge
Display of inadequacy

Ask the students to think of some examples of each type of misbehavior. (It is helpful to prepare some of these examples on a ditto sheet before the class meeting.) Students are asked to clarify the behaviors according to type. These discussions can be especially useful when certain behavior problems crop up in school—for example, lying, stealing, disrupting classes, failing, and committing acts of vandalism.

Tell the students to match the following four messages with the appropriate goal of misbehavior. In other words, ask them what message is being communicated by the behavior. (The appropriate answers are given in parentheses.)

"I want to be the boss." (power)
"Look at me. I want you to notice me!" (attention)
"Leave me alone and don't ask me to do anything, because I can't do anything right." (display of inadequacy)
"You hurt me, and I want to hurt you back." (revenge)

Ask the students how these messages are communicated to others. Here are some of the more common ways:

Attention getting: disrupting class, teasing people, being loud, and asking many unnecessary questions.
Power struggle: arguing with people all the time over almost anything, especially with parents and teachers.
Revenge seeking: stealing, telling lies, calling names, fighting, and destroying others' property.
Display of inadequacy: doing nothing right, not trying to do one's best, intentionally failing in schoolwork, breaking things, and having accidents.

Ask the students to match the following feelings they may experience when people direct the above misbehaviors at them with the probable goal of the misbehavior. (The appropriate answers are given in parentheses.)

"I feel hurt." (revenge)
"I feel annoyed." (attention)
"I feel threatened." (power)
"I feel helpless." (display of inadequacy)

Have the students role-play some situations involving each of the four goals of misbehavior. Scenes may be from home, school, or any other situation. Encourage the students to develop appropriate and helpful ways of dealing with these behaviors. Here are some examples:

Display of inadequacy: encourage and help the person to succeed.
Revenge seeking: listen to the person's feelings and thoughts and become his or her friend.
Power struggle: refuse to argue or fight; walk away.
Attention getting: ignore the behavior.

The success of the discussion will depend on how effective you are in drawing additional thoughts, feelings, and opinions from the students. An interesting follow-up activity is to investigate ways of finding one's place that don't infringe on the rights of others as they seek to find their own place.

A second follow-up activity is to list on the board three student misbehaviors or types of irresponsible behavior. Ask the group to pretend that they are the parents of the children who engage in such behaviors and to rank the behaviors from the most to the least serious. You may wish to select the three misbehaviors from the following list:

Shoplifting	Cheating in school
Dropping out of school	Promiscuous sex
Drug abuse	Fighting

Ask students to suggest other misbehaviors. Be sure to follow up the class rating of the three misbehaviors by asking the students why they ranked the behaviors the way they did.

Activity: The Motives of Our Behaviors

Level: Grades 3-6

Purpose: To develop awareness of why we behave the way we do by examining our emotional reactions and aggressive behaviors. All behavior is caused by some need or needs we are trying to fulfill (refer to the four goals of misbehavior). When we can't meet these needs, we may feel quite frustrated and take aggressive action. People may behave differently because they have different needs and because they tell themselves different messages about what happens to them. That's why ten people may react in ten different ways to the same event.

Procedure: Ask for volunteers to role-play a group of students rushing to get in the cafeteria line. After the line is formed, have one boy come in late and try to crowd into the front of the line. Tempers flare, and two boys begin fighting. Come over to the line, stop the fight, and assign detention to both boys.

Following the role playing, ask the class to tell what happened and why they think it happened. You may wish to consider some of the following questions for discussion:

1. Why do some students want to crowd in and be first in line and others don't?

2. Why do some students try to stop crowders and others don't?
3. Why didn't everybody try to be first?
4. Which goals of misbehavior were the two fighters trying to achieve?

A follow-up discussion with the group leads into a discussion of individual differences in the ways people behave and of the goals of such behaviors. During the discussion the students will probably mention that being first in line is one way to feel important. Encourage the group to suggest other ways to feel important that don't infringe on the rights of others and that don't get us in trouble.

A helpful homework assignment is to have the students write in a daily notebook all the aggressive acts they see themselves and others do over the next three to five days. This type of assignment can be made more interesting by asking the students to assume the role of newscasters and report their findings on a video- or audiotape to be used later in class for discussion. Keep in mind that some of the terms used in the study of human behavior—such as *behavior, needs, emotion, frustration,* and *aggression*— may need to be clarified for the students.

Activity: Learning about Behavior Patterns

Level: Grade 4-Adult

Purpose: To become aware of our own patterns of behavior as well as those of others; to examine how these patterns are different for different people; to provide strategies for dealing with others whose behavioral patterns and work styles are different from ours.

Procedure: Introduce the idea that we all need to be able to cooperate with others and that sometimes people's behaviors and work styles conflict with one another. For example, some people may be very businesslike and efficient in getting their work done, while others may tend to be just the opposite. If two such people find themselves working together, a difficult situation may develop.

You may want to stress to your group that people do have reasons for behaving the way they do. Noisy people may be noisy because they are bored, frustrated, tense, or just starved for attention. People who don't seem to pay attention may not understand, or may not want to understand, what is going on and what is expected of them. People who avoid participating in group activities may do so because they can't do the work as quickly and as well as the rest of the group.

With the cooperation of the group, write on the board a list of the various ways in which people work or behave in group situations. For each mode of behavior listed, write down its opposite. For example:

Some people tend to be:	Other people tend to be:
noisy	quiet
quick	slow
careless	careful
followers	leaders
sidetrackers	goal directed
uncooperative	cooperative
sad	happy
serious	carefree

After your lists have been developed, select one pair of behavioral modes and divide the group into two smaller groups according to how they characterize themselves on the two dimensions chosen. For example, you may have those who tend to be leaders in one group and those who tend to be followers in another group. Arrange the two groups into an inside and outside circle. The inner group is invited to discuss why they behave the way they do, while the outer group listens and observes. (The group interaction seems to be more effective when members talk about their own behavior style rather than the general behavior of the group.)

After the members of the inner group have had a chance to speak about their own modes of behavior, ask them to tell the others how they feel about those people who behave just the opposite of them. When the inner group has finished discussing these two topics, have the two groups switch places and repeat the process. Discuss as many of the behavioral modes and their opposites as time and group interest allow.

It is a good idea for the participants to devote the last few minutes of the activity to sharing what they have learned about others who behave differently from them. If you are dealing with a large group, you may want to divide it into smaller groups of two, four, or six for this summary discussion.

Activity: Tattling

Level: Grades 1-3

Purpose: To find out what tattling is and to determine when it is helpful and when it is not. Tattling generally involves some kind of negative communication about a co-worker or peer to a person in authority. Since the primary goal of tattling is self-enhancement, the goal is achieved by downgrading others to authority figures in order to make oneself look better by comparison. Tattling may be the lazy person's way to achieve strokes or positive reinforcement. The message of the tattler may be "I don't have to achieve much myself if I make everybody else look bad."

There are instances, however, in which tattling may be both self-enhancing and helpful—for example, when it is done in self-protection or to protect others or the environment and it does not result in destructive behavior.

Procedure: Begin your discussion by writing the word *tattle* on the board. Have the younger students practice the correct pronunciation of the word. Ask each student what the word means to him or her. Write the students' definitions on the board and then consult a dictionary and encyclopedia for additional information on the origins of the word.

Some dictionaries point out that the verb *to tattle* was used as early as the 1500s to describe the meaningless cackle of a bird. Some encyclopedias contain descriptions of the tattler—a type of sandpiper with a long bill and a loud, clattering call.

Next, ask the group to recount instances of tattling in which they were personally involved and to explain why the tattling was or was not helpful.

Activity: Personality Chains

Level: Grades 4-6

Purpose: To become aware of different personality characteristics and the possible motivations behind some behaviors; to develop empathy for those toward whom one's behavior is directed; to solve classroom problem situations.

Procedure: Ask the group to suggest some behavior problems that occur in school — fighting, lying, cheating, stealing, name calling, and so forth — and list them on the board.

Choose a group of four students and ask them to sit in a semicircle facing the rest of the class. After deciding which problem situation they want to role-play, ask them to assign themselves the roles of the various protagonists and recreate the situation as it generally happens at school. Avoid playing the "blame game" by talking about who really did what to whom and when. Instead, have the students focus on how others think and feel when the problem occurs.

After role-playing the scene, lead the whole group in a discussion of the students' reactions to the scene—especially how they think the situation should be handled. Sometimes it is helpful to point out the three role transactions that occur in some of the "bad games" that people often play: the persecutor, the victim, and the rescuer. During these "bad games" the roles can change quickly. The persecutor may suddenly find himself or herself being the victim; the rescuer, the persecutor; and the former victim, the new rescuer. Such a switch in role can happen, for example, when a well-meaning rescuer tries to break up a fight and ends up becoming the target of both fighters' anger.

In this activity, too, it is a good practice to ask the group what the role players were trying to get by their behavior and whether they were successful. Lead the group to evaluate the role-playing behaviors by asking them in what ways the different behaviors were helpful or not helpful.

If your group has had little or no experience in role playing, it is helpful to practice some short verbal and nonverbal types of role playing as warm-up exercises and confidence builders. For example, you may begin your meeting by having everyone stand up in a circle, with one person leading an exercise such as jumping jacks. After a few seconds, select another leader for a new exercise. Another good warm-up activity for role playing is to ask the students to show how they:

1. Walk in deep snow,
2. Walk through a mud puddle,
3. Walk through leaves,
4. Eat an ice-cream cone,
5. Eat cotton candy,
6. Suck a lemon,
7. Play catch with another person,
8. Toss a hot potato (or a feather, or an egg) back and forth with another person in the group,
9. Could be a mirror image of someone in the group getting ready to come to school—washing one's face, brushing one's teeth, combing one's hair, and so on,
10. Carry on a phone conversation with an imaginary friend,
11. Introduce people to each other.

Activity: Self-Descriptions

Level: Grades 4-6

Purpose: Self-awareness and awareness of classmates' personalities.

Procedure: Have the students write on a sheet of paper five key words or phrases that describe their personalities through feelings, interests, and self-concepts or values. Tell the students not to put their names on the papers. Examples of self-descriptors are: "I am likable," "I am capable," "I am good at doing math problems," "I am not good at doing math problems," and "I don't have any friends."

Read the descriptions from each paper in turn (without mentioning names) and ask the class to suggest three other things each student might have added to his or her list. For example, for the student who said "I am likable," the class may add "I have a lot of friends," "I treat others well," and "I don't start fights."

If there is time, go back through the lists and ask the class to guess who wrote what and why. This important feedback exercise helps the students become aware of how others see them. There is no need for you to identify who actually said what. The important thing is that the students know how their personality and behavior affect others.

Most group leaders who do this activity find that students are able to identify who said what about himself or herself. However, as we said earlier, there is no need to confirm these guesses.

Activity: Our Needs and Our Individual Differences

Level: Grade 5 and up (with modifications)

Purpose: To learn and understand the meaning of our tangible and intangible needs and to examine how each of us tries to meet these needs.

Procedure: Ask the students to define the word *needs*; then have the group discuss and make a list of things we need. When the list is complete, ask the students to classify these needs into one of the two broad categories of physical needs and emotional needs. If the level of your class permits, have the students classify the needs into Maslow's (1970) hierarchy of human needs:

> Self-actualization needs[1]
> Self-esteem needs
> Love and belonging needs
> Safety needs
> Physiological needs

---

[1]The need for self-actualization, the highest of all human needs, may be defined as the need to become all that one can become.

Activity: Meeting Our Needs through the Roles We Play

Level: Grade 5 and up (with modifications)

Purpose: To help participants achieve a sense of identity through role playing and to develop a sense of appreciation for how others feel in their roles.

Procedure: Lead a class meeting on the topic of how we meet our needs through the roles we play. How many roles do we play? Why do we change the roles we play? Do we all play the same roles? What are some of these roles? For example:

1. Boy Scout/Girl Scout
2. Son/daughter
3. Student
4. Friend
5. (Others)

Ask your students to consider how their roles help them meet their needs or goals. Ask them also to consider whether their roles conflict with their goals or whether their goals or needs conflict with one another.

As a follow-up activity, ask the students to make the chart illustrated in Figure 4-1. The students put their names in the center of the innermost circle and list their needs inside the middle circle and the roles they play to meet these needs in the outside circle.

Activity: Group Dynamics

Level: Grade 5-Adult

Purpose: To examine what makes a joint effort successful and how each group member may contribute toward the group endeavor; to find out what makes a good group leader and a good group member; to stimulate creativity in the classroom and to appreciate the rewarding experience of working in a good group.

Materials: Poster board, crayons, Magic Markers, rubber cement, old magazines, and scissors.

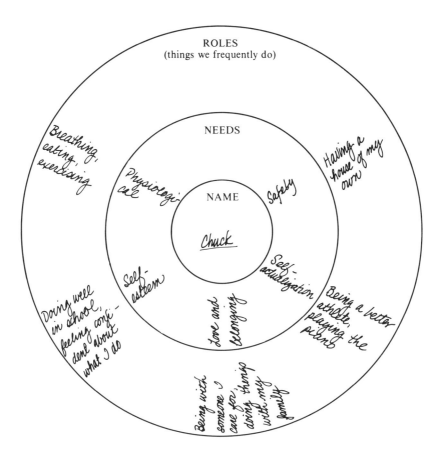

ROLES
(things we frequently do)

NEEDS

NAME

Chuck

Figure 4-1. Needs and roles chart.

Procedure: Have the class select a subject that can be rendered into a symbol on a poster board or on wrapping paper. The class may select a topic they are studying, the school itself, one of their club activities, a current event, the community, a career area, or any other topic of interest. Divide the class into groups of five or six and provide each group with poster board, crayons, Magic Markers, rubber cement, old magazines, and scissors. It is always helpful to have around a sample symbol made by a previous group, so the class can see what they are supposed to do. However, any coat of arms, flag, state seal, or trademark can serve the purpose if the symbol's parts are explained to the groups.

Inform the groups that they have 15 minutes to complete the symbol for the subject they have chosen. After 10 minutes, call time out and ask the groups to analyze what has been going on in their group by answering the three questions you have written on the board:

1. Is everybody in your group participating?
2. Whose ideas are being followed?
3. How is your group deciding what to do?

Let the groups spend about five minutes answering the above questions. You may choose to print the questions on ditto paper to allow group members to respond without being influenced by the perceptions and feelings expressed by the others. Complete agreement among group members would be as interesting as complete disagreement.

When the five-minute analysis period is over, tell the group that they have five more minutes to complete their symbol. Call another time-out at the end of the work session and ask the groups to repeat their previous analysis period, answering the three questions again. Note any changes in their responses between the first and the second analysis periods.

Conclude the activity by posting the symbols around the room. Ask each group to explain their symbol and how they worked together to design and produce it.

Activity: Who Is Missing?

Level: Grades K-4

Purpose: To establish a feeling of belonging and a sense of identity and to develop awareness of the importance of having friends who notice us.

Procedure: Ask the students to look around and see who is here today. Darken the room and ask the children to put their heads down and close their eyes. Walk around the room and lead one child out of the room. Turn on the lights and ask the group to find out who is missing.

Repeat as long as the interest remains high. (Never wear out any of your activities by overuse.) If the group should fail to notice who is gone, congratulate the "winner" and ask the others how he or she was able to fool them. Follow up your discussion by asking these questions:

1. How do you feel when nobody notices you?
2. When someone is left out, what can you do to help?
3. How do people get other people to notice them?
4. How do you get your teacher to notice you? Your parents? Your friends?

5. Do you know everybody in here well enough to miss them when they are not here?

Activity: Group Series

Level: Grades 4-6

Purpose: To provide children with the experience of how it feels to be on the inside and on the outside of a group.

Procedure: Place six chairs in a small circle inside a large circle. Tell a secret (real or imaginary) to the six children who make up the inside group. The children in the outer circle have five to ten minutes in which to find out the secret by asking questions. "Insiders" may give as many clues as they desire and may choose to control the behavior of the "outsiders" by ignoring them and their questions if their behavior becomes disruptive. (A point for discussion is that people often choose to become disruptive when they feel that they don't belong—that they are outsiders.)

After the allotted time period, six new children form the inside circle and are given another secret, and the process is repeated. The sequence may be continued as long as interest remains high.

The discussion phase is the most significant part of the activity. Ask your students to consider the following questions:

1. How does it feel to be on the inside as compared to being on the outside of a group?
2. Did you enjoy keeping others outside your group?
3. How do you keep people outside a group?
4. If you don't like being on the outside, are you still planning to keep other people there? Why? Why not?

This activity provides some good empathic experience for those students (class leaders) who are always on the inside and for those isolates who never get there.

Activity: Role Playing

Level: Grade K-Adult

Purpose: To help solve problems involving conflict with others; to teach assertive behavior and interpersonal skills through rehearsal and practice; to liven the curriculum; to develop empathy for another person's point of view; to teach group and problem-solving skills.

Procedure: Although role playing has appeared in several other activities in this book, we have chosen to describe its various steps to ensure that teachers will develop expertise in the use of such an effective teaching aid.

Teachers begin to involve their students in role playing when they ask them to put themselves in the place of some famous character and to behave the way they think the character behaves (or behaved). The students are encouraged to identify as much as they can with their roles, so that they almost think and feel like the character they are playing. The teacher often brings up a significant decision the person being role-played had to make and asks the role player what he or she would have done.

All of this is an introductory form of role playing and leads to the next stage, in which a group of students is involved in actual role playing of dramas. In some cases students prepare skits for presentation to their class and other classes. At other times the role playing is spontaneous. The scenes reenacted by the students range from historical and current events or literary works to classroom, school, and home problem situations. It is a good idea to have a student director responsible for keeping the action moving. Audiences seem to be most involved when they have the privilege

Role playing with puppets provides a medium for expression of feelings and thoughts in the counseling setting.

of "tapping in" on the role of any character in the drama or skit — that is, when they are permitted to express their own thoughts and feelings through one of the characters in the skit. Frequently conversations are going on between two (or more) members of the audience — all speaking through the characters in the skit.

A preliminary consideration in using role-playing activities is how to get started. If you have ever experienced anxiety at a party over playing charades or some other "acting-out" game, you will be able to identify with the many children who are very anxious at the thought of being asked to role-play. Because role playing is a frightening risk for many, it is necessary to build confidence and reduce anxiety.

First of all, help the students warm up to role playing. Begin by asking them to role-play some of the simple situations mentioned earlier in this chapter. Be sure that each member of the class has a chance to be involved in this warm-up activity. Also, encourage the class to reinforce one another for their efforts. Applause is appropriate if it is not disruptive.

Here are some examples of simple nonverbal role playing:

1. Eating various things:
   toasted marshmallows, candy apples, ice cream, sour pickles, watermelon, tough meat, spaghetti, hot soup, taffy, or bubble gum.
2. Walking through or on things:
   mud, snow, ice, leaves, water, sand, high grass, railroad tracks, marbles or stones (barefoot).
3. Doing things with others:
   a. play catch with a ball, a hot potato, a feather, a Frizbee, a balloon full of water, or an egg;
   b. be a mirror image of somebody getting ready to go out for an evening or just getting ready to go to school;
   c. teach someone how to swim, row a boat, hit a golf ball, or swing a baseball bat.

Simple role-playing exercises using verbal interactions can include:

1. Two people carrying on a telephone conversation
2. One person introducing a friend to another person
3. Radio or TV reporter interviewing someone
4. Job interviews
5. Officer ticketing a driver for speeding
6. Taking back a defective appliance to the complaint department of a department store

After some warm-up exercises the class will probably be ready to begin working on role-playing scenes dealing with real problem situations or conflict interactions in their everyday life. Some typical scenes include cheating on tests, stealing, crowding in line, and fighting.

To begin, the "director" and the audience set the scene, choose their role players, and start the action. The whole scene may last only a few seconds but should be long enough to stimulate group discussion about the role players' feelings and thoughts. Frequently alternative approaches to the problem are role-played. The key to role playing is the discussion it fosters, which may result in helpful changes of behavior.

It is a good practice to save a little time for getting the class' response to each role-playing session. An evaluation procedure will help the counselor or teacher keep in touch with the students. Role playing provides students with the opportunity to learn new behaviors, practice them in low-risk situations, and apply them in situations outside the group. A typical role-play script might go as follows:

> *Mary:* Bill, may I copy your math assignment? I didn't get mine done last night.
> *Bill:* Well, I don't know about that. I really worked a long time to get mine done.
> *Mary:* Oh, come on! How would it hurt? I'll let you copy my problems for tomorrow.
> *Bill:* Well, I guess it might be OK. . . . But suppose we have a test over the problems we copied from each other and we can't do them. Won't the teacher know we didn't do our own work?
> *Mary:* Oh, Bill, come on! Let me have your paper; we don't have much time!
> *Bill:* Well, OK I guess.

Ask your students to tell how Mary and Bill were probably feeling (don't forget to ask Mary and Bill also). Invite the group to make a value judgment about Mary's and Bill's behaviors. How was copying helpful to Mary? How was it helpful to Bill?

If the whole class or some of the students agree that copying the problems was not helpful, ask what Bill and Mary could have done. Ask the students what they would have done if they had been Bill or Mary.

Other role-playing activities include role-playing the outcome of open-ended stories and filmstrip stories and the use of puppets. A final comment: even poorly done role playing provides a welcome change of pace to most students.

Activity: Open-Chair Role Playing

Level: Grade 2-Adult

Purpose: To help teachers enhance their skill in the use of role playing in group settings and to help students develop new ways of behaving in problem situations.

Procedure: A difficult task in class meetings is maintaining group involvement while one or two of the participants are engaged in role playing. Another problem is that some students are reluctant to role-play a personal concern because they fear too much self-disclosure. Open-chair role playing can help maintain group involvement and can serve as an intermediate procedure to move students from merely talking about themselves to actually role-playing themselves. When properly used, this activity can help the group focus on common problems and build group trust and cohesion.

The first step is to introduce a hypothetical person to the group by labeling an empty chair with the name of someone whose characteristics are similar to those of many of the class members. For example, a sheet of paper with the name Tracy is taped to the chair while the group leader says "Here is Tracy, a 7-year old student much like many of you. Let's list on the board some of the problems Tracy may be facing this year." After the list has been compiled, the participants vote to determine which particular problem they would like to discuss. Once the problem has been identified, the group can be involved in writing a situation for role playing. Each role-playing situation should detail the issue, the situation, the characters (usually two), the time, and the place. Anything else deemed necessary may be added. For example, if the problem under consideration is Tracy's

Fear of participating in role playing can be reduced by having three students play each role.

telling a friend she wants to stop their friendship, the issue would be "friends" and the characters would be Tracy and, say, Bill, a friend of nearly a year. The time could be tomorrow evening at the playground.

The procedure for role playing consists of labeling two chairs "Tracy" and "Bill." (A piece of paper with the name written on it is actually taped to each chair.) The chairs remain empty, and three role players sit on the floor beside each of the empty chairs or in three other chairs placed immediately behind each of the empty chairs. Whoever wants to start may do so. The three students role-playing each of the two characters may say whatever they think would be appropriate. Role players don't need to agree on what type of role they are playing, nor do they need to jointly plan what they will say. The students should take turns, saying what they think would be appropriate for the situation.

All other group members are asked to observe the role playing and identify the aspects they like or dislike. After five or six minutes of role playing, you may interrupt with an open statement such as "Well, what are your reactions?" Ask the class members to state what aspects of the role playing they found helpful or unhelpful. Ask what they wish had happened but didn't. This question may lead to another role-playing situation, which is a variation of the one just preceding it.

Resource:
Value Explorations through Role-Playing, by Robert C. Hawley (New York: Hart, 1975), presents many modifications and variations of open-chair role playing.

Activity: Effective Complaining

Level: Grade 4-Adult

Purpose: To teach some basic communication skills involved in making effective complaints; to teach the difference between being assertive and being aggressive; to teach the importance of making effective complaints as opposed to sanctioning an undesirable behavior or action by not complaining.

Procedure: There are several guidelines one may follow in making effective complaints. The guidelines the counselor or teacher selects should be in part determined by the learning level of the students. Fewer and more concrete guidelines are taught to younger children, and the degree of abstractness generally increases with the age of the students. The basic procedure is to distribute a list of the guidelines to the students, defining their meaning in terms of behavior, and then discuss any questions the students pose.

Following the discussion, students are asked to select a partner with whom to practice the new guidelines. One of the two partners plays the role of the complainer and the other one that of the person against whom the complaint is lodged. The students are asked to think of a recent occasion in which they made a complaint or didn't make a complaint when they should have. In role-playing the situation, each partner tries to follow the guidelines when it is his or her turn to complain.

Here are some of the guidelines (Thompson & Poppen, 1972):

1. Complain to whoever is infringing on your rights and no one else. Frequently many of us complain to everyone but the right person, with two possible consequences: (a) the people causing you trouble never hear the complaint, and (b) they keep doing the same undesirable behaviors.
2. Avoid comparisons with others. Do not say "I wish you were as good as the teacher I had last year." Rating a person as inferior brings an end to listening and a beginning of defensive behavior.
3. Make your complaints as soon as it is feasible to do so. Repressing bad feelings caused by resentment is not especially helpful to anyone.
4. Make just one complaint at a time. Do not confuse the issue at hand. Avoid saying "And furthermore. . . ."
5. Give people a chance to correct their behavior (if possible) before going on with the complaint. For example, if people crowd in ahead of you in a line waiting for the movies, ask them if they are aware that the end of the line is back there.
6. Sarcasm has no place in effective complaining. If used, the result may be that your complaint is taken as a joke and not heeded or you may further damage a relationship without having your complaint heard.
7. Refrain from asking people "why" they do things when you mean to say "Stop doing it." If you ask why, the person may tend to rationalize the undesirable behavior and continue to do it. Just ask people to *stop* the behavior!
8. Rehearse your complaints in order to avoid unhelpful complaining behaviors.
9. Be sure to make your complaints if you consider them to be legitimate. Failure to make your legitimate complaints gives the green light for continuing infringement on your rights. Even if the person does not respond to your complaint, you will be stronger for having informed the person of your limits.
10. Ask yourself what is the worst possible thing that could happen to you

if you make the complaint. Developing the courage to complain may be the hardest thing to do, because sometimes we may tell ourselves all sorts of ridiculous things that will happen if we make the complaint. Unfortunately, worse things seem to happen when we do not make the complaint.

Activity: Cooperation in Problem Solving

Level: Grade 5-Adult

Purpose: To help students become aware of how their behavior may help or hinder group problem solving. To demonstrate the importance of cooperation in group problem solving.

Materials: Puzzles (see below) and envelopes.

Procedure: The procedure used in this activity originates from materials developed by the National Training Laboratory Institute, Bethel, Maine, and published in *Today's Education* (NEA Journal), October 1969, page 57. The activity begins with an open-ended discussion on the meaning of cooperation and the ways in which cooperation can be used in group problem solving. The following points on effective group problem solving need to be brought up:

1. Each group member needs to understand the problem.
2. Each group member believes that he or she has something helpful to contribute.
3. Both self and others need to be considered.
4. Instructions must be clear to each member.

Form small groups of five members each. Describe the problem to be solved by each group, pass out an envelope containing a puzzle and an instruction sheet to each group, and read the directions aloud (see instructions below). After clearing up any questions about the instructions, give the signal to open the envelopes. When all or most of the groups have solved the problem (completing five squares), call time and discuss the experience.

Ask the members to share how they felt when someone who held a key piece to the puzzle didn't see the solution. Also, find out how the group felt about those who, having finished their own puzzle (completing one square), sat back without bothering to see whether their puzzles contained some pieces the others needed to complete the remaining four squares. It is helpful if the counselor or teacher can relate this exercise in cooperation to the functioning of the group as a class on a day-to-day basis.

General instructions

Each person should have an envelope containing the necessary pieces to form squares. At the signal, each group tries to form five squares of equal size. The task is not complete until everyone has before him or her a perfect square. All the squares must be of the same size. These are the rules:

1. No member may speak.
2. No member may ask for a card or in any way signal that he or she wants one.
3. Members may give cards to others.

Instructions for making the puzzle

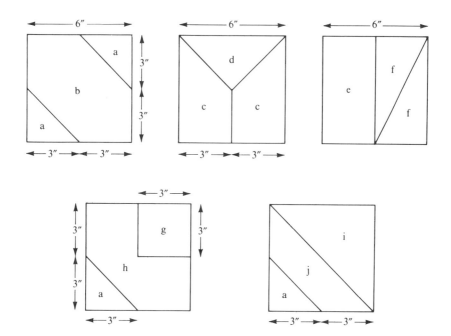

Each group receives five envelopes, each containing the following pieces:

Envelope A: e, h, i
Envelope B: a, a, a, c
Envelope C: a, j
Envelope D: d, f
Envelope E: b, c, f, g

Write *A* on all pieces contained in envelope A for reuse. Do the same for the other four envelopes.

Activity: Getting to Know You

Level: Grade 1-Adult

Purpose: To encourage students to become better acquainted with one another at the beginning of the year; to help students to listen to one another and communicate the messages they hear to the whole group; to develop confidence in sharing thoughts and feelings with the group.

Procedure: Divide the group into dyads. Choose as partners students who don't know each other or don't know each other well. The members of each dyad are asked to introduce their partner to the group. Younger students tell the group their partner's name and one thing about him or her—preferably something that the group doesn't already know and that the partner agrees to share. The counselor or teacher can model the process by asking "Do you know everybody in our class yet?" "How well do you know everybody?" "If I said that there is someone here who broke his arm when he was 2 years old by falling off a tree, would you know who this is?"

The activity can be modified as follows. Have the group sit in a circle on chairs or on the floor. It is important that the participants be able to see one another. Explain to the participants that they are about to learn the names of all the participants. Tell them to try to remember everyone's name because they are going to be asked to repeat as many names as possible. Proceed around the circle, having the students introduce themselves and repeat the names of all of those who have been introduced before them. If the group is too large, reduce the number of names to be remembered by forming smaller groups.

Another variation is to have the students recall the last three names before their own and then introduce themselves. For example, Jan says "I'm Jan"; Bill says "This is Jan, and I'm Bill." Have members change places in the circle and ask for volunteers who can name all the other members. Children enjoy this activity. If the children are well acquainted with one another, have each child state his or her name and mention one thing he or she likes or enjoys. Then, as they proceed around the circle, the participants recall the name of each child and what that child likes or enjoys.

Occasionally the counselor or teacher may want to use mnemonic devices to help the children recall the others' names—rhymes, alliterations, and catchwords are some of the devices that can be used. Care should be exercised to prevent students from having their feelings hurt. Therefore the leader explains that a whistle will be blown on words that make fun of others. Acceptable examples are:

Cheerful Charlie	Raggedy Ann Ruth Ann
Sharing Sharon	Avis Mavis
West Virginia	Bouncing Betty
Tan Jan	Dollar Bill
Jumping Jacque	Exxon Ethel
Fan Us Janice	Fancy Nancy
Rapid Robert	Hammering Henrietta

Activity: Student Orientation

Level: All grades

Purpose: To orient new and transfer students to their new school and to help them feel welcome.

Procedure: The following steps are applicable to new students enrolling in a school in the fall as well as transfer students enrolling during the year:

1. After registration compile a list of the new students.
2. Have the new students tell about themselves and their former school in a group discussion. You may want to use the partner's-introduction activity described in Getting to Know You (above).
3. Meet two or three mornings for 30 minutes with new student groups to go over school handbook, policies, and so on.
4. Follow up with students' individual counseling as needed.
5. Tour the building and go over schedule of library, guidance, physical education, and lunch.
6. Assign "buddies" to new students for the first day or two. These buddies should be chosen among students who have the same schedules—that is, who ride the same bus and attend the same math or reading groups.
7. Check with the teacher the following week to determine whether the students appear to have adjusted.

Activity: Getting to Know about You

Level: Grade 2-Adult

Purpose: To increase children's ability to communicate meaningfully in a short time.

Procedure: Post the following list where everyone can see it (on the board or on a large sheet of paper taped to the wall):

1. Something you both like to do
2. Something you both agree on
3. Something the two of you have in common

    Form an outer and an inner circle, each composed of six members. The two circles should be facing each other. Point to the list and say "Talk with the student in front of you about one or all of these things. You have three minutes." Every three minutes the inner circle rotates in a clockwise direction until all the members have talked with each other. Then the whole group discuss their feelings and thoughts about:

1. How they felt about changing partners so rapidly,
2. The most difficult thing about changing partners so often,
3. How they felt if they found someone who was hard to talk with and why it was hard to talk with him or her,
4. What could be done to make it easier to talk with this student.

Activity: Graffiti

Level: Grades 4-6

Purpose: To give students a chance to express their feelings and thoughts on any topic they wish; to provide the students with an opportunity to know how others are feeling and thinking.

Materials: Several large sheets of paper (could be butcher paper).

Procedure: Tape the sheets of paper to the wall and encourage the students to write their graffiti there rather than on other school walls. You may wish to set some ground rules about profanity and name calling. Suggest that, in writing their graffiti, the students follow the rule of commenting only on those personal characteristics that can be changed.

    Acceptable topics would include how one feels about oneself, others, school, and the world in general. Student thoughts on how things should be done are welcomed. Jokes, rhymes, and funny comments have a place in the activity as do satire, artwork, and cartoons.

After the graffiti sheet has been up for a week, the class may want to have a classroom discussion on the feelings and thoughts expressed in the graffiti. Sometimes expression of feelings and thoughts can lead to productive action plans.

Activity: Helping Oneself by Helping Others

Level: Grades 3-5

Purpose: To have students discover the tangible and, eventually, the intangible rewards of helping and being kind to others.

Materials: Construction paper (all colors) and the pattern of a tree.

Procedure: The activity is most successful with small groups of six to eight students and should be attempted only after a few discussions on friendship and the values of friendship. All students are provided with enough brown construction paper to make the tree trunk and limbs. (The number of limbs, the same for everybody, should be decided by the instructor on the basis of the level of the class.) Each child will write his or her name on the trunk of the tree, glue the branches to the tree, and tape it to the wall or on the bulletin board. The students will then use construction paper to cut out leaves of different colors (the number is established on the basis of the number of branches used). All the leaves will be placed in a box, and, as each student does a "good deed," he or she picks up a leaf and glues it to his or her tree. Before the students can add a leaf to their tree, they must tell the group of the good deed in question and the group must agree that it was indeed a good deed. When the children have completely filled their trees, they may receive a reward.

Discussion will revolve around the good deeds done by the participants. Students should be helped to understand the value of doing something for others, the value of friendship, the needs of others, and the needs of oneself. This is a very good exercise for students who appear to be withdrawn, because it helps students develop a sense of self-confidence.

Activity: Self-Expression

Level: Grades 1-3

Purpose: To help students express themselves more freely and feel more at ease when talking to a group of people.

Materials: Tape recorder.

Procedure: Demonstrate the use of the tape recorder by recording your own voice. Play back. Ask the students to imitate an animal and tape the imitations. Play back. Then let the students tell something about themselves and their family and listen to the playback. Ask the students about ideas they would like to discuss on the tape.

Activity: Sex Education

Level: Grade 6-Adult

Purpose: To teach some basic sex-education concepts and to answer students' questions about sexuality.

Procedure: The following steps represent one way of conducting the program:

1. Parents are informed of the class and invited to preview the material.
2. Parent-permission slips are filed in the counselor's office.
3. Filmstrips — one for boys and one for girls — are shown to segregated small groups by the guidance counselor.
4. Question-and-answer sessions are conducted by the counselor.
5. Individual student/counselor sessions are provided.

The following sample evaluation instruments are to be used to evaluate pre- and postprogram knowledge of sex information.

Sex-Education Unit

Evaluation: Girls

Write "T" by the statements that are true and "F" by the statements that are false.

_____ 1. Hormones will assist your body in changing and maturing into adulthood.
_____ 2. It is not unusual for maturing boys and girls to be somewhat chubby for a while.
_____ 3. My menstrual cycle is 40 days.
_____ 4. When I start menstruating at school, I must go home and stay home for a week.
_____ 5. I cannot swim, play ball, or wash my hair during my menstrual period.
_____ 6. I can have a baby as soon as I have my first menstrual period.
_____ 7. Boys undergo a periodic physical change similar to menstruation in girls.
_____ 8. I can have a baby without really having sexual intercourse with a boy.
_____ 9. The ovaries release an egg every 28 days.
_____ 10. The egg waits 20 days before it leaves the body.

Evaluation: Boys

Write "T" by the statements that are true and "F" by the statements that are false.

_____ 1. Hormones will assist your body in changing and maturing into adulthood.
_____ 2. It is not unusual for maturing boys and girls to be somewhat chubby for a while.
_____ 3. Wet dreams will keep me from growing.
_____ 4. My voice changes because my neck gets too long.
_____ 5. The girls are taller because they eat more.
_____ 6. Hair on my face and under my arms is a sign I can father a baby
_____ 7. My first sign of puberty is the growth of my testicles.
_____ 8. Deodorant helps keep the odors of perspiration from becoming obvious.
_____ 9. When girls menstruate, they are not well and can't do anything.
_____ 10. Girls like boys who act cute and show off in class.

Resource:
About Sex and *Growing Up*, two filmstrips by the Society for Visual Education (1345 Diversey Parkway, Chicago, Ill. 60614).

Activity: Individual Decision Making in a Group Setting

Level: Grade 3-Adult

Purpose: To use group discussions to arrive at several possible alternatives to personal decisions.

Materials: 3 x 5 cards.

Procedure: Ask the members of the discussion group to write on a 3 x 5 card a brief description of a decision or concern about which they need help. Place all cards face down on a small table or chair in the middle of the group. Proceed through the following:

1. If any member wants to go first, he or she will tell the group about the decision on his or her card.
2. If not, the leader turns up one of the cards and asks the member who wrote it to read and explain the decision to the group.
3. The participants listen carefully and then take turns asking clarifying questions of the person concerned.
4. Everyone in the group writes on a 3 x 5 card one positive suggestion for dealing with the decision. Suggestions may concern action to be taken before making the decision or may deal directly with the course of action dictated by the decision. Each person then reads and explains his or her suggestion. When all suggestions have been made, the cards are given to

the group member concerned for his or her consideration. If the group is very large, the cards are simply given to the student concerned, who retires to another part of the room to read over the cards while the group deals with another concern. A second meeting may be held the next day to continue with the next step.

5. The group member concerned selects three cards containing the suggestions that he or she thinks are most helpful. The reasons for the choice are then discussed with the group.

This procedure can be modified for use in group decision making. First, the members of the group agree about the problem and write it in specific terms on the blackboard. Next, the group members write suggestions on cards. The suggestions are written and tallied on the board and discussion follows until a decision is made or a consensus is reached.

Activity: Class-Council Meetings

Level: Grades 3-12

Purpose: To have students form their own government as a means of resolving class conflicts, reevaluating class rules, dealing with unusual situations, and planning for class activities.

Procedure: The class council may be instituted if and when the teacher thinks that the students are capable of conducting themselves in a democratic manner. Two or three students are elected by the group to conduct the meetings. Any of the traditional election procedures can be adapted to elect the class officials. It should be kept in mind that the election is not meant to be a popularity contest; it is a means to select those who will conduct the class-council meetings. These elected officials will replace the teacher as group leaders during class-council sessions. New leaders are chosen frequently (every two or three weeks is recommended with younger students) to give all students an opportunity to lead the group. The time periods should be predetermined so that students will know the duration of their term and no sudden elections will be necessary.

Class-council meetings are scheduled at regular times. During the meetings students can bring up matters that concern them, such as problems and suggestions for class activities. The teacher can also bring up topics for discussion. If the class has a suggestion box, the council meeting may be a regular time to examine suggestions that have been submitted.

The teacher participates as a member of the group, although in early meetings he or she may need to exercise quite a bit of control to ensure that some students do not dominate the meetings and that all students are given the opportunity to express their opinions and concerns.

As in class discussions, it may occasionally be necessary to stop the meeting and wait until all the students are paying attention. In some cases the teacher may call a special class meeting to discuss problems that have developed within the council.

If at first class-council meetings do not seem productive, it should be kept in mind that students need time to develop the necessary leadership and group-membership skills. However, if after several meetings the group still seems incapable of conducting class-council meetings, it may be that the students are simply not ready for this activity and may feel more comfortable and secure in their own contributions to the group when meetings are conducted by the teacher.

In some instances the class council may be used to deal with discipline situations not covered by the normal rules. If so, the teacher should maintain a veto power to ensure fairness.

Resource:

Maintaining Sanity in the Classroom: Illustrated Teaching Techniques, by R. Dreikurs, B. Grunwald, and F. Pepper (New York: Harper & Row, 1971).

Chapter Five

ADULT/YOUTH RELATIONSHIPS

One important area of focus for school guidance programs is the improvement of child/parent and student/teacher relationships. The rationales for such focus are:

1. Existing problems in this area negatively influence the overall school atmosphere.
2. The resolution of parent/child conflicts has positive effects on students' learning.
3. Providing individual and group counseling on personal relationships is one of the primary skills of school counselors.
4. Experience indicates that counseling is effective in promoting good human relationships.
5. The promoting of effective human relationships can be accomplished efficiently with groups of students, teachers, and parents.

If there is anyone on the school staff who possesses the skills necessary to promote supportive human relationships, that person is the school counselor. School counselors not only have training in counseling but are generally familiar with group dynamics and parent education. These skills and knowledge are essential for achieving the goal of improved adult/youth relationships.

The following section focuses on activities aimed at improving adult/youth relationships at home, in school, and in the community.

Activity: Orientation Program

Level: First-graders, transfer students up to grade 6, and their parents

Purpose: To organize and present an orientation program for first-graders, transfer students, and their parents as a way of facilitating adult/youth relationships.

Materials: Story or filmstrip, refreshments, school bus (with driver).

Procedure: As soon as the new students' addresses are known, they and their parents are invited by letter to attend an orientation meeting. Radio announcements can be issued and broadcast on the local station(s). The meeting should be scheduled for a day and a time that are as convenient as possible for the parents. One of the project center's orientation meetings was scheduled for a Thursday afternoon, when stores and businesses were closed, and from 3:30 to 4:30, so that parents who worked in factories could attend.

Name tags are made, and the children are registered as soon as they arrive. The first-grade teachers take the students on a tour of the building and have a story-reading session or show a filmstrip in the first-grade room while counselor, principal, and school nurse meet with the children's parents. The children are also introduced to the school-bus driver, who, after talking briefly with them, takes them for a ride around the block. Later the children go through the cafeteria line and carry their refreshments on trays to the tables, just as they will be expected to do once school starts. The parents' response to the orientation program is usually very positive. (See the questionnaires for parents of first-grade and transfer students—Instruments 9 and 10—in Appendix C.)

Activity: Orientation

Level: All levels

Purpose: To expand the orientation program.

Procedure: In an effort to expand the high school orientation program, one of the project centers decided to have high school students talk to the eighth-grade classes. Different students were invited to the various classes. An effort was made to choose students who were fully aware of the different opportunities offered by their high schools (clubs, organizations, athletic opportunities, and extracurricular activities). The eighth-grade students related well with the high school representatives and seemed to become more confident about going to high school.

Generally this is a successful way of introducing younger students to high school. The project center's orientation program also included a visit from the high school counselor at the beginning of the school year to all the eighth-grade classes. Other useful orientation activities are class meetings with the elementary school counselor to discuss the students' concerns about high school, individual discussions with the counselor, the principal, and the teachers about schedules for the freshmen year, and a trip to the high school in the spring.

Many counselors conduct parenting-skills groups.

Activity: Imaginary Home Visit with Dolls

Level: Grades K-1

Purpose: To help the counselor have a better understanding of the child's home background and to help the child consider and discuss conflicts at home or problems about school attendance.

Materials: Bend-a-Doll Family (flexible play dolls).

Procedure: Begin by helping the student to make a floor plan of his or her home and label the various areas of the house (kitchen, bedroom, and so forth). Drawing a stove in the kitchen or a bed in the bedroom will help very young children identify more easily the rooms in the floor plan. Next, pretend to be a visitor to the child's home and have the student describe the various rooms and their contents. Encourage the child to move the dolls from room to room as he or she tells about the family. You can speak for the various family members in order to engage the student in acting out dialogues with them.

You may also ask questions to determine what happens in the child's home during a typical day—for example, "Who gets out of bed first?" and "Who eats breakfast?" Bedtime and weekend activities can also be enacted by both you and the child by moving the dolls around and speaking for them.

This activity is especially useful for those children who have problems with their parents, brothers, or sisters. By acting out the various situations, the child may come to see how his or her own behavior contributes to the situation and, by rehearsing new approaches, he or she may find solutions to the problems. Finally, this activity may permit you to notice, perhaps for the first time, interests and potentials the student may not be using at school.

Resource:
Bend-a-Doll Family (Order No. 3286; Miles Kimball, 41 W. Eighth Ave., Oshkosh, Wis. 54906).

Activity: Divorce Discussion

Level: Grades 4-6

Purpose: To help students who come from broken homes or who have problems with their stepparents; to help students find solutions to some problems caused by the divorce of their parents.

Materials: "Once-a-Month Mother," a story in the *Value Series.*

Procedure: Use the story as a stimulus for group discussion about the problems that divorce may cause for children. Ask your students to come up with possible solutions to the problems presented in the story. This technique, which creates a climate of empathy among students, often helps children who ordinarily don't participate in class discussions to become open and informative. In leading the discussion, make sure that the students keep to the topic of the story and that the activity doesn't become a discussion of the students' personal problems. Students who do have problems about divorce at home shouldn't bring them before a class or should do so only after they have had an individual interview with the counselor. The relevance of this activity lies in the fact that it deals with a topic that seems to be a neglected and sometimes even avoided area of children's problems.

Resource:
"Once-a-Month Mother," a story in the *Value Series: Values to Learn*, by V. C. Arnspiger, J. A. Brill, and W. R. Rucker (Steck-Vaughn Company, Box 2028, Austin, Texas 78767).

Activity: Skit

Level: Teachers or parents

Purpose: To present a humorous yet realistic fashion parade of teachers' or parents' types.

Materials: The script was adapted by the project personnel from the article "If the Shoe Fits," which appeared in the September 1969 issue of *Today's Education*. The cast was made up of teachers from various schools, primarily the guidance committee of the project-center school.

Procedure: The guidance committee and other cast members met and planned the skit. Only one 30-minute rehearsal was held. The guidance committee had previously presented a skit for in-service training that was based on Ginott's book *Between Teacher and Child*. A supervisor asked whether the guidance committee could come up with a similar performance for the first morning of in-service training. The program received many favorable comments from the teachers.

Resource:
"If the Shoe Fits," *Today's Education*, September 1969. (Reprints are available from the National Education Association, 1201 16th St., N.W., Washington, D.C. 20036.)

Activity: Case-Conference (C-Group) Meetings

Level: Parents or teachers

Purpose: To help parents or teachers deal more effectively with "problem children."

Procedure: Form a group of parents or teachers (8 to 12 people) who feel that group meetings and sharing may be helpful to them. The usual format for these meetings is a problem-solving approach combined with the use of the communication skills presented in Sax and Hollander's book *Reality Games.*

During the problem-solving phase of the meetings, the group focuses on the individual member's concerns until each person has had a chance to present his or her problem. Then the group practices the communication skills. The training for such skills is described in the first chapter of *Reality Games.* The members follow a process of:

1. Identifying a problem of one of the group members;
2. Describing what has been done and what is being done to solve the problem;
3. Evaluating present and past problem-solving behaviors;
4. Brainstorming for alternatives;
5. Predicting outcomes of alternatives;
6. Attempting a new approach (including rehearsals and role playing);
7. Reporting outcomes to the group;
8. Recycling the process if necessary.

Since the C-group combines case study and communication training, many participants report that the group experience has helped them with their problems and has also resulted in personal growth.

Resource:
Reality Games, by S. Sax and S. Hollander (New York: Macmillan, 1972).

Activity: My Favorite Teacher

Level: In-service education for teachers

Purpose: To help teachers become more aware of their students' needs.

Materials: Mimeographed handouts.

Procedure: The school counselor should set aside approximately one hour for the following:

1. Present a lecture-type talk about "the teachers we've known and loved" and what made them lovable.
2. Hand out the following questionnaire and ask each participant to fill it out in private. (Allow ample time, but don't overdo.)

Questionnaire

a. Briefly describe your favorite teacher.
b. Briefly describe a teacher you disliked.
c. What did teachers do that made you feel bad?
d. What did you see teachers do that made students feel bad?
e. What did teachers do to help you develop confidence and security?
f. What did teachers do to you that made you feel insecure or unimportant?
g. What did teachers do to help you feel important?
h. What do people generally do when they are afraid or insecure?
i. What do people generally do when they feel good about themselves?

3. Read the first item in the questionnaire and list some of the volunteered responses on the chalkboard; continue the process through each item or question.
4. Which of the negative behaviors described in the responses are behaviors we have engaged in ourselves? Lead a discussion on this important point. Also discuss the positive ways of dealing with students described in the participants' responses.

Resource:
Workshop in Nashville, Tennessee, conducted by Dr. Ralph H. Ojemann, Director of the Educational Research Council of America (Rockefeller Building, Cleveland, Ohio, 44113).

Activity: Get-Acquainted Name Tags

Level: Grade 3-Adult; in-service for teachers

Purpose: To encourage teachers, parents, and students to get to know one another.

Materials: Magic Markers, 4 x 8 cards (or cut standard construction paper in half), tape or pins.

Procedure: Each person is given a name tag—that is, a 4 x 8 index card or a piece of construction paper of the same size. In the center of the card the person writes his or her first name in large letters. The counselor then gives directions so that each person can complete the rest of the name tag. When completed, the tag should look somewhat like the one illustrated in Figure 5-1.

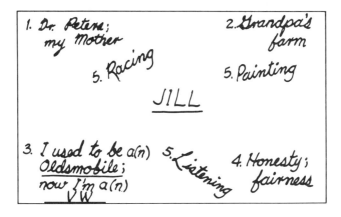

Figure 5-1. Name tag.

1. In the upper left-hand corner of the name tag list the two people who have greatly influenced you.
2. In the upper right-hand corner write the name of the place where you spent the happiest period (any length of time) of your life.
3. In the lower left-hand corner fill in the blanks "I used to be a(n) _____; now I'm a(n) _____." Use anything you want (animals, cars, cities, or whatever).
4. In the lower right-hand corner write two values that are important to you.
5. Scattered somewhere on the tag, write three words that describe you as a person. All words must end in *ing*. For example, you might write *teaching, loving,* and *swimming.*

After the name tags have been completed, the group members are asked to inspect one another's name tags without making comments. The participants might want to shake hands or in some other way greet one another. The counselor then asks the participants to walk around and choose two other people with whom they would like to talk. Groups of three are formed and given a discussion topic—for example, "Something that has made you feel very happy" or "Some decision you've made recently that made you feel good."

After a few minutes the counselor directs the participants to form new trios. With young children or reluctant participants, the counselor can give each person in the trio the number 1, 2, or 3. The participants stand up and raise the number of fingers corresponding to their number to find a new partner with the same number. When three 2s or three 3s are together, a trio is complete and a new discussion period begins, in which a new topic is assigned to the trios—for example, the two values or some other item listed on the name tag.

This is an excellent activity for the first day of school. It is also a good way to open a PTA meeting. Teachers and parents discover interesting aspects about one another. Participants generally find that people have many common interests and experiences.

Resource:
Decisions and Outcomes: A Leader's Guide, by H. B. Gelatt, B. Varenhorst, R. Carey, and G. Miller (New York: College Entrance Examination Board, 1973; Introduction).

Activity: Public-Relations Exhibit

Level: Adult

Purpose: To prepare a guidance exhibit for a district fair in one of the project-center communities. The guidance exhibit was part of an educational exhibit sponsored by the local education association. The overall objective was to improve the school's image by bringing to people's attention some of the school's educational accomplishments.

Materials: Burlap was used for the background. Letters and large jigsaw-puzzle pieces were cut from corrugated cardboard and painted by members of the high school art department. Handouts were prepared.

Procedure: A committee composed of six high school counselors and one elementary school counselor planned the exhibit. Later six teachers from the project-center elementary school volunteered to help plan and carry out the exhibit.

There was a large tent with exhibits from each department in the school. The guidance department asked for the last booth and used the theme "Guidance Puts It All Together." The five areas of focus in the Title III Guidance Program were developed for the theme. The five areas were: student self-concept development, effective peer relationships, career awareness, academic progress for all learners, and good parent/teacher/student relationships. Each major objective of the guidance program was depicted as a large jigsaw-puzzle piece.

One of the most gratifying things about the project was the fact that members of the project-center school volunteered to help plan and carry out this display.

Activity: What Does It Take to Make It?

Level: Students, teachers, and parents

Procedure: During this small-group activity all participants should try to answer as specifically as possible the question "What does it take for a student, teacher, or parent to be a success?" The group (which includes some teachers, some students, and some parents) may talk about any of the three roles first, but sooner or later all three roles should be discussed. The discussion should go through the following five phases:

1. Students, teachers, and parents talk about what it takes to be successful in their respective roles. A recorder should take notes. The leader focuses the discussion on the specific skills that each group member thinks are needed to be successful.
2. The roles are reversed; each person takes another's role, and the discussion continues. For example, each teacher or parent takes the role of student, and each student takes the role of parent or teacher.
3. After the roles have been reversed for some time and different viewpoints have been presented, the group discusses what they have learned from playing a different role. All members should evaluate the role reversal as helpful or unhelpful.
4. A list of what it takes to be successful as a student, teacher, or parent is compiled, discussed, and accepted by the group.
5. On the basis of the data collected, group members select a behavior they would like to try before the next week's follow-up meeting. Written commitments to try the new behavior can be left with the recorder. At the follow-up meeting the group members report on the outcome of their new behaviors.

Participants report increased empathy as a result of their experience and a clearer understanding of self-expectations and the expectations of others. The activity is quite useful for a class whose members have doubts about course requirements, rules, and so forth. The sentence-completion form "Attitudes toward Others" (Instrument 11) in Appendix C can be used to evaluate this activity.

Activity: Guidance Report to Parents and Teachers

Level: Grades 4-12

Purpose: To let the parents know how the students feel about the guidance program and to keep them informed of the effects of the program.

Procedure: Periodically (about every 12 weeks) administer the questionnaire below to randomly selected students or classes. Tabulate the results and send the parents a report based on the data obtained.

Student Questionnaire

Write "Yes" or "No" in the blanks.

_____ 1. The guidance meetings have helped me understand myself and my feelings better.
_____ 2. The guidance lessons have helped me learn to solve my problems more effectively.
_____ 3. The guidance meetings have helped me understand why people sometimes act as they do.
_____ 4. My parents know we have a counselor.
_____ 5. The counselor is interested in everything we do at school.
_____ 6. The counselor works with the teachers.
_____ 7. The counselor is here to help me.
_____ 8. The counselor is interested in all the pupils, not just the ones with special problems.
_____ 9. I feel free to discuss with the counselor things that matter to me.

Put a check by the problems that you would feel free to discuss with the counselor.

_____ personal problems   _____ difficulties with a teacher
_____ family problems   _____ identification of career interests
_____ problems with schoolwork   _____ others (please list)
_____ boy/girl relationships   _____
_____ study habits   _____

How would you describe your counselor?
_____ friendly   _____ interested in me
_____ helpful   _____ bossy and preachy

Put a check by the activities or items you wish your guidance program used more frequently.

___ filmstrips	___ games
___ talks by parents	___ stories
___ role playing	___ small groups
___ tape recordings	___ field trips
___ outside speakers	___ classroom meetings

A questionnaire may also be used to determine the teachers' attitudes toward the services offered by the guidance program. Giving the teachers feedback concerning the popular and the unpopular aspects of the program can lead to fruitful discussions and to improvement in the whole school atmosphere. (See Instrument 12 in Appendix C.)

Activity: Volunteer Aides

Level: High school-Adult

Procedure: Distribute the Volunteer-Help Sheet to all interested parents.

Volunteer-Help Sheet

Dear Parent, High School Student, or Interested Citizen,

We need your help. In order to provide the best education for our children, we need to offer a wide range of experiences for them. You have hobbies, interests, skills, and experiences that can be of help to the school. Please indicate what you would like to do for the school.

___ 1. Listen to children read aloud.
___ 2. Demonstrate a hobby or craft to a small group.
___ 3. Help individual children learn basic skills.
___ 4. Help with preparing materials, typing, pasting, cutting, and so on.
___ 5. Other (please list):_____
___ I am not interested at this time, but I will be interested later.
___ I am interested. I can come for ___ 45 min. ___ 60 min. ___ 90 min.
    other: _____
Mon. ___   Tues. ___   Wed. ___   Thurs. ___   Fri. ___
___ I am interested, but other obligations prevent me from volunteering my help.
___ I can come once to demonstrate a skill or craft.

Your name _____
Your telephone _____

Yours truly,

Primary Unit Teachers,
Fourth Grade Teachers,
Guidance Counselor

Community volunteers are a valuable asset to the guidance program.

When the "Unicorn" activity was carried out at one of the project centers, it created considerable interest and involvement among the students. The entire activity was almost totally and directly the result of the efforts of community volunteers. The following account, filed by the elementary school counselor, "tells the story."

This is the first year of the Unicorn at Greenbrier Elementary School. Inspired by the enthusiasm of the third-graders and their art teacher—who fashioned a Winnie-the-Pooh character from wire, paper, paste, and paint—Mrs. Evelyn Ehrenwald, a volunteer worker, created the Unicorn. Her friends, as well as other people in the community, watched the birth of the Unicorn from gallons of wheat paste, hundreds of pounds of old newspaper, an old fence of poultry wire, and many coats of paint. Both students and teachers now reckon time by saying "Oh, such and such an event happened during the summer when the Unicorn came." The Unicorn now has a permanent home on the balcony of the school library with the other fantasy characters.

A naming contest was held for the Unicorn (sponsored by the student council). A dedication exercise announced the name and station of the Unicorn to the school community. The Unicorn was named Unae (pronounced Uni). Much research was done by the students to find out who created the fantasy creature—the Unicorn. Mrs. Ehrenwald wrote a beautiful poem, "The Dance of the Unicorn," which was read over the intercom. The students listened and wondered whether the Unicorn might magically jump from the balcony and start dancing. The Unicorn can be seen dancing on a still night only by those who truly believe that it lives. The poem "The Dance of the Unicorn" follows.

The Dance of the Unicorn

My friends don't believe me
When I tell them I saw
A beautiful Unicorn, white as the snow,
Come in my yard, while the stars were still bright,
Come and then linger most of the night.

He came just as quiet as a soft, winter snow,
But where he went I never did know.
One cool, summer night, he appeared on my lawn,
And I watched him and watched him
Almost 'til dawn.

He picked at the grass and drank from the spring,
Then suddenly I saw him give such a swing
I knew he was dancing on the green, grassy lawn.
He danced on his toes, glistening like gold,
While his well-rounded horn, as sharp as a thorn,
And the tip of his tail, like a smooth, soft sail
Curved and waved in the pale moonlight.

He looked like a cloud come straight from the sky,
And there for a moment I thought he would fly.
He leaped on the hill, then took a broad jump
And pranced on his heels without even a thump
In the cool, summer night.

If the animals who live in the forest below
Could talk, they would say it is certainly so
For they stirred in their sleep, and came out to see
What in the world the trouble could be
In the quiet night.

They stood very still
And gazed at the hill,
While the Unicorn's feet
Gave a magical treat to us all.
Then quick as a beat, they were loosed from their sleep
And began to dance at the Unicorn's feet.
They hopped and they skipped in a circle around
Then turning did it all over again.
They danced and danced in the cool summer night,
They danced and pranced in the pale moonlight.

A squirrel hung by his tail from a tree,
And a rabbit perched on a high stump to see;
A mockingbird, whirling, lit on the Unicorn's head
And trilled such a song—it's all like I said—
So sweet and so clear
I feared that the neighbors, alarmed by the sounds,

Might call a policeman to come from the town.
But the dancing kept going—on and on—
It continued for, oh, I don't remember how long.
But I think—well, I know—it was very near dawn,
For at the first streak of daylight
The Unicorn was gone.
He vanished away in the blue-grey light;
He was carried away far out of my sight.

So when my friends tell me the story is not so
I tell them a story told long, long ago—
The Unicorn can most certainly be seen
But only by those, who truly believe
That he lives.
And I tell them a Unicorn did come my way,
He came in my yard while the stars were still bright,
Came and then lingered most of the night.
He danced and danced in the cool summer night,
He danced and pranced in the pale moonlight.

Published with permission of the author, Mrs. Evelyn Ehrenwald.

Chapter Six

ACADEMIC ACHIEVEMENT

Academic achievement is another area of considerable interest in the school guidance program. Although the students' academic performance is primarily the teachers' responsibility, such responsibility is shared not only by the students themselves but also by their parents and other significant adults. Whether a student succeeds or fails is very much a result of the interplay between the school and the home environments. Both can significantly help or hinder the student's efforts to become academically responsible and successful. Facilitating academic achievement is, therefore, a high-priority function of school counselors. Such a function is performed by

1. directing the coordinated efforts of students, teachers, and parents toward realistic academic goals,
2. helping the students understand their academic behavior and finding ways to increase their performance,
3. consulting with the appropriate personnel to improve the school's learning climate.

The following strategies for students, parents, and teachers are designed to correct some of the problems that interfere with academic achievement. Instruments 13 and 14 in Appendix C can be used to assess changes in study habits on the part of those students who have received instruction on effective study methods.

Activity: Tutorial Programs

Level: Grades 1-12

Purpose: To involve high school students and parent volunteers in the elementary school guidance program as tutors; to improve the academic achievement of those students identified by the school staff as needing tutorial assistance.

Teachers with large numbers of students have little time to give individual attention to those pupils who are doing badly and who seem to care little about doing better. The tutorial program is based on the assumption that both tutor and student benefit from the tutorial relationship (Thompson & Cates, 1973). The tutor learns by teaching, and the student benefits from the one-to-one teaching/learning relationship.

Procedure: Several types of tutorial programs may be initiated in the school. Consider the following tutorial arrangements:

1. Parent volunteers
2. College student volunteers
3. High school student volunteers
4. Upper-level students tutoring lower-level students
5. Low-achieving students from middle-school grades tutoring low-achieving students in the primary grades
6. High-achieving students tutoring low-achieving students in the same grade

The most effective tutorial programs are those that the counselor or other school staff members closely supervise. Careful and thorough selection of tutors and students is quite important, and so is the matching of students and tutors for compatibility and effectiveness. Many times matching has to be done on a trial basis to find out who works best with whom. Following selection and matching, it is recommended that the details of the tutorial program be spelled out in student/tutor contracts.

A key factor in the smooth administration of tutorial programs is the accurate scheduling of appointments and the accurate record keeping of the number of hours logged. Therefore, it is necessary to have a signing-in and signing-out procedure to record what is happening. A simple card file will do the job. Tutors sign in and out and total their service hours for each session. Points for tutoring can be built into some of the programs. Students and adults participating in service clubs may earn service points by contributing time to the volunteer tutoring programs. Points and rewards for in-school tutors may also be arranged by the counselor. Points count toward free time or other activities the students may find rewarding. The student's progress is the best reward if the progress is recognized by the school staff in the form of phone calls, notes, or Happygrams to the parents, students, and tutors.

Peer-tutoring projects help increase student achievement.

The following guide is typical of some of the aids counselors may prepare for adult tutors. This particular guide emphasizes several excellent points for tutoring the beginning reader. These and other good ideas for teaching reading and language arts in the elementary school may be found in Ruth Robinson's (1960) book *Why They Love to Learn* (p. 21).

1. Pronounce each word clearly and have the children repeat the words after you while keeping the place with their fingers.
2. Show children how to move their fingers from word to word.
3. Repeat the same words as many times as you deem it necessary. Do this politely.
4. Praise the children when they read a word correctly without help.
5. The most difficult words for children to master are the short words that

Tutor Contract

Date _____

To Whom It May Concern:

_____ agrees to work under the direction of
(Name of student-tutor)

_____ helping children with learning activities
(supervising teacher's name)

on _____ from _____ to _____ in the
(days of the week)   (time)   (time)

_____ class at _____ School.
(name of class)   (name of school)

We have read and we agree to the above terms beginning _____
(date)

and ending _____. The tutor's reward for satisfactory performance
(date)

of tutoring duties will be _____ .

Signatures:

Tutor _____

Tutor's Parent(s) _____

High School Principal _____

Elementary School Principal _____

Supervising Teacher _____

Supervising Teacher _____

Counselor _____

Volunteer-Tutor Program

Your name _____

Address _____ Telephone _____

Check one: Parent _____ Student _____ Other _____ Grade (if student) _____ look so much alike—for example, *this, that, them, than, there, they, these, those, which, what, when, where, in, if, it, is, at, as, an, saw,* and *was.*

6. Children should not be forced into long periods of reading. From three to five minutes is a good start.
7. Reading should be fun. It should be made easy and pleasant so the children can succeed and enjoy it. Don't let them fail. Be generous with praise!
8. When the students don't know a word, tell them, don't test them!

Resource:
Why They Love to Learn, by R. Robinson (Charlotte, N.C.: Heritage Printers, 1960).

Activity: Grade and Behavior Contracts

Level: All grades

Purpose: To provide students with clear and concise descriptions of what it takes to do well in school; to help students commit themselves to a plan of action and to follow through on their commitments; to make the classroom a place where students want to be; to improve student academic performance and behavior.

The project counselors who adopted the contract approach found it most useful in helping student and teacher determine the right level of learning and in matching the student's stage of cognitive development with work that is neither too difficult nor too easy, and therefore boring, for that stage. Contracts also provide opportunities for students to exercise choices in selecting ways to meet performance objectives in their school subjects. A situation in which the student is responsible and accountable for his or her own learning appeals to many students. Contracts also help to eliminate the "failure atmosphere" prevalent in many classrooms, because the emphasis is on skill development rather than on some form of letter grading. Finally, contracts offer second chances to pass.

Perhaps contracts serve their best purpose when they function as a road to achievement. Built-in recognition of improvement in academic tasks and behavior is a significant part of a good contract. A final word of warning: no contract will succeed if students see the academic tasks as meaningless.

Procedure: Several types of contracts were used in the project. The following is an example of a *Level-1 Contract,* which utilizes a point system that allows students to earn free time and credit toward a grade (adapted from Thompson, Prater, & Poppen, 1974).

Level-1 Contract

Class Behavior	*Points*
1. Walking into classroom on time, without running	1
2. Checking out work folder	1
3. Asking teacher or aide for daily assignment	1
4. Reporting to the teacher or aide with completed assignment	1
5. Checking and correcting work (no points are earned for incorrect work)	1
6. Working without disturbing others	1
7. Achieving at least 70% accuracy on each worksheet	1
8. Returning folder to file	1
9. Leaving room quietly, without running	1

100 points = 30 minutes free time

Student's signature _____
Teacher's signature _____

This Level-1 Contract provides for free time that the students earn by completing individualized daily assignments. For example, by collecting a total of 100 points, the student earns 30 minutes of free time. The system is organized so that each student can earn approximately 10 points per class period. Free time may be spent as the student wishes. A screened-off free-time area in the room offers a selection of activities—checkers, chess, comic books, novels, painting equipment, puzzles, play dough, various games, and even rope jumping (if shoes are removed). Students may also bring their own games.

The contract makes clear that the students can do what they want during their free time. There is only one rule: students engaged in free-time activities cannot bother those who are working. If the rule is broken, the remainder of the free-time period is forfeited and 200 points (instead of 100) must be earned by the student for another 30 minutes of free time. Points are deducted at the rate of one point per offense if the student prevents another student from working. When a child is engaging in disruptive behavior, the teacher or aide signals the student by raising one finger to indicate the loss of one point. Each student's point total is charted for the day, and the students are informed of both their total for the day and their running point total. Students are motivated by receiving daily feedback on their performance and by observing their classmates enjoying free time.

The *Level-2 Contract* is a teacher's "proclamation" of what it takes to do well in the class. The student has no choices in the assignments and

These three young men are displaying their pocket contracts for the coming school week.

receives no points for good behavior. The goal of the Level-2 Contract is to eliminate any ambiguity about what students need to do to pass or make an "A" in the class. Therefore, assignments and learning activities are spelled out in such a way that the students have no doubts as to what is required of them.

The *Level-3 Contract* is similar to the Level-2 Contract, with one important distinction: it lets the students propose alternatives to the teacher's plan for passing the course or for earning a specific grade. These contracts are negotiated and may be renegotiated up to an agreed point in time.

The *Level-4 Contract* is a contract for independent study and is proposed entirely by the student. The proposal must answer four basic questions:

1. What do you want to learn?
2. How are you going to do it? What are your resources and procedures?
3. How are you going to report what you have learned and when?
4. How are you going to evaluate what you have learned?

This type of contract encourages creativity, in-depth learning, and responsibility. To become a valid agreement, the contract must, of course, meet both parties' standards.

Merit-Badge Contracts are organized much like those used in Scout merit programs. Learning tasks for each subject area are identified, and the students work on each task until they feel ready to pass that particular "badge." If they pass, the date of the test is written beside the task. If they don't, nothing is written and the students do some more work before trying the test again. The advantages of the Merit-Badge Contract are obvious: students work at a comfortable pace of their own choosing; the pressure is not so great; and students, parents, teachers, and counselors all have a record of what skills the student has mastered.

Resources:

"Reporting Student Progress: A Case for a Criterion-Referenced Marking System," by J. Millman (*Phi Delta Kappan*, December 1970, pp. 226-230).
For Those Who Care: Ways of Relating to Youth, by C. Thompson and W. Poppen (Columbus, Ohio: Merrill, 1972).

Merit-Badge Contract for Mathematics

Skills	*Date*

Concepts
 Understands commutative property of addition (for
  example 4 + 3 = 3 + 4) _____
 Understands place value (for example, 27 = 2 tens + 7 ones) _____
Addition
 Supplies missing addend under 10 (for example, 3 + ____ = 5) _____
 Adds three single-digit numbers (for example 2 + 3 + 4 = ____) _____
 Knows combinations 10 through 19
 Adds two 2-digit numbers without carrying (for example,
  14 + 11 = ____) _____
 Adds two 2-digit numbers with carrying (for example,
  14 + 16 = ____) _____
Subtraction
 Knows combinations through 9 _____
 Supplies missing subtrahend under 10 (for example,
  6 – ____ = 1) _____
 Supplies missing minuend under 10 (for example,
  ____ – 3 = 4) _____
 Knows combinations 10 through 19 _____
 Subtracts two 2-digit numbers without borrowing (for
  example, 14 – 11 = ____) _____
Measurement
 Reads and draws clocks (up to quarter hour) _____
 Understands dollar value of money (coins up to $1.00 total) _____
Geometry
 Understands symmetry _____
 Recognizes congruent plane figures—that is, figures that are
  identical except for orientation _____

Skills	*Date*

Graph reading
Knows how to construct simple graphs _____
Knows how to read simple graphs _____

Pocket Contracts are little cards with a daily schedule that the various teachers initial when the student meets the terms of his or her grade or behavioral contract (see Figure 6-1). This type of contract is especially helpful for specific behaviors the student is trying to change, such as missing class, being late, fighting, and not completing homework.

	(Teachers' Names)				
Date	Smith	Adams	Gibbs	Jones	Logan
9/27	*L. L.*			*m. y.*	*a. g.*	
9/28					
9/29					
9/30					
10/1					

Child's Name: _____   Total Points _____

Figure 6-1. Pocket Contract.

If, for example, the student makes it through the class period without fighting, the teacher initials the card. At the end of the week the student brings the card to the counselor for his or her short weekly report.

The card could also be used with a point system, but generally a positive weekly report is sufficiently reinforcing in itself, especially when the student gets a little positive attention from all the teachers every day.

Survival Contracts are designed for students who haven't been able to succeed in any of their school tasks. Often several months go by before any effort is made to assist those students who seem doomed to failure. The Survival Contract represents an agreement between student and teacher that will earn the student a minimum pass for the year in exchange for mastering some basic skills consistent with the student's level of academic achievement. In those cases in which teacher and student have "behavioral problems," the contract can also include terms covering both the student's and the teacher's behaviors. Walter may agree not to fight with the other students, and the teacher may agree not to nag Walter when he does. If

Walter breaks the agreement, he may be directed to a time-out room. Whatever the agreement, the Survival Contract will spell it out in clear and unequivocable terms.

Daily Point-Sheet Contracts are for students (generally younger students) who need immediate reinforcement. Each child is given a sheet divided into squares (see Figure 6-2). When each square has been checked by the teacher, the student can trade it for a reward. Checks are awarded for completing an assignment successfully, working out a tough math problem, receiving a good grade, or answering correctly in class. The teacher gives the checkmarks according to how much a particular task is worth and how much encouragement a particular student needs. Rewards for a completed sheet could range from sugar-free candy and gum to free time. Generally the goal is for the student to earn a page of checks in one day's time.

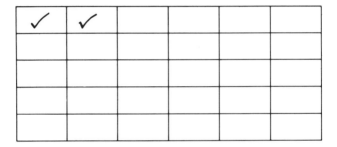

Figure 6-2. Daily Point-Sheet Contract.

Activity: Book Sharing

Level: In-service for teachers at all levels

Purpose: To expose teachers to a different technique of learning.

Materials: An expendable textbook or paperback related to the topic your class is studying; a room large enough for people to mill about.

Procedure: The counselor should allow about 45 minutes for the following series of steps:

1. Tear out one page of the book for each teacher. Distribute the pages among the teachers.

2. Allow five to ten minutes for the teachers to read their page.
3. Have each teacher select one or two statements on their page that they would like to share with one other teacher. Allow a few minutes for such sharing to take place.
4. Have the teachers exchange pages with one another and repeat the procedure of sharing information with a different partner.
5. Exchange pages again and share with three others, then with six others. Call time.
6. Form a circle and have each person share with the group one thing they have learned.
7. Ask the following questions:
   a. Was this a useful way to learn new ideas?
   b. Can it be tested?
   c. Can it be used in the classroom?
   d. How do you feel about it?
   e. Do these sample pages make you want to read the rest of the book?

Activity: Daily Travel Log

Level: Grades 3-8

Purpose: To turn a vacation trip into an educational and enjoyable learning experience.

Procedure: The February 1973 issue of *Learning* (Vol. 1, No. 4) presented 11 suggestions to teachers interested in having their students keep travel logs of their vacations and later report to the class. Here they are:

1. Keep a daily diary of trip activities.
2. Maintain a record of expenses. Include what is spent for transportation, food, lodging, and other items.
3. Chart the route of the trip on a map. Note the places you have visited and keep a mileage chart.
4. Interview different people along the way and write a summary of the interviews in the log.
5. Draw a sketch impression of the places you have visited.
6. Collect postcards and souvenirs along the way.
7. Make a list and drawings of the different types of plants and animals you have observed during the trip.
8. Construct a day-to-day temperature graph. Record the high and low temperatures for each day. Which day showed the greatest range?
9. If you had a specific destination, time the trip going and returning. What was the variation and why?

10. Describe the colors you observed along the way. What does each color bring to your mind?
11. If you had been to the same place or places before, describe how this visit was different from the previous one(s).

A vacation trip can become an enjoyable learning experience that can be shared with others.

Activity: Reinforcement for Reading

Level: Grades 1-6

Purpose: To motivate students to improve their reading level.

Procedure: Students are given "token chains" to hang on the wall. Each time students do well in some reading assignment (such as completing worksheets, reading in class, and correcting their own mistakes on the worksheet), they receive a token to hang on their chain. Ten tokens may be exchanged for 30 minutes of free time. Tokens may also be earned for perfect performance on flashcards and for spelling words correctly.

Activity: Creative Writing

Level: Grades 4-12

Purpose: To provide students with an opportunity to express themselves through art and writing and to offer a different approach to teaching language arts.

Procedure: Place students in a circle around a table. Provide each student with a poster square, a pencil, and a piece of paper. Place coloring equipment on the table. Ask the students to draw pictures of their favorite places and to write a short story about their drawings. Time permitting, an interesting discussion could follow the completion of the task, focusing on individual reactions to the experience. Discussion topics may include:

1. Do the students' favorite places have something in common with one another?
2. If they don't, how do they differ?
3. What does a student's choice of a particular spot tell us about the student?

Activity: Hangman

Level: Grades 1-6

Purpose: To learn new words and to improve one's ability to work as a member of a team.

Procedure: Choose a word. Draw on the chalkboard as many dashes as there are letters in the word to be guessed. For example, if the word is *paper,* you draw five dashes: _ _ _ _ _. The children begin by asking whether a particular letter is in the word—for example, "Are there any *a*s? Any *c*s?" and so on. Each time a student suggests a letter that is not in the word, you say "No" and draw a portion of the "gallows" or of the "victim" on the board. Look at Figure 6-3. Start at number 1 and follow all the way to number 14. Begin your drawing at the platform and proceed upward.

This game is generally a big success. Students learn to "sound out" the mystery word from the first letters guessed correctly by the group. The game also helps children learn to work together by taking turns in asking questions. When the students have progressed enough, they can use words they have chosen themselves in advance for the activity.

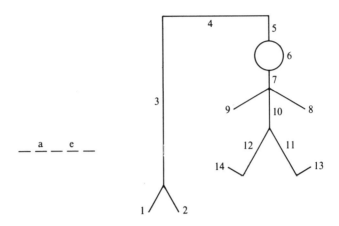

Figure 6-3. The Hangman.

Activity: Learning to Tell Time

Level: Grade 2

Purpose: To motivate students to learn how to tell time.

Procedure: Conduct a classroom discussion on the following questions:

1. Why do we need to know how to tell time?
   Responses might include: to know when to go to school or to work, when to leave home to be on time for an appointment, when to watch TV, and when to catch a bus.
2. What do we need to know before we try to tell time?
   Responses might include: numbers 1 through 12; how to count by 1s and 5s; what the numbers 3, 6, 9, and 12 stand for in a clock; where each number belongs; the meaning of *o'clock, quarter past, quarter of,* and *half past;* that the two hands of the clock are of different sizes and that they mean different things; what we mean when we speak of minutes and hours; that number 1 stands for five minutes, number 2 stands for ten minutes, and so on; how to distinguish left from right; the concepts of small and large.
3. Why didn't you learn to tell time before?
   Responses might include: I was too young; I didn't understand all about numbers.

Let the students work first with manual clocks or toy clocks such as the Teach-a-Time guidance toys. When the students have mastered manual clocks, shift to real watches.

This activity was one of those that the project counselors used to demonstrate the importance of breaking learning tasks into their simplest components. Whenever possible the counselors facilitated the identification and utilization of mediational learning experiences in the classroom.

Activity: Concept Analysis

Level: Grade 1-Adult

Purpose: To develop a procedure for diagnosing the students' level of concept understanding.

Procedure: Before presenting a lesson, ask several students of different abilities to describe what a particular concept, such as magnetism, means to them. After writing their responses on the chalkboard, conduct a short class discussion to find out the extent of class agreement, disagreement, or confusion about the concept. The activity can be used individually or with the entire group. You can plan the learning activities related to the key concept by building lessons on the related terms and definitions already known to the class. The concept-analysis discussion, if conducted in an active manner, can motivate the students to learn more about the concept. The teacher who becomes competent in concept analysis will feel in greater control of his or her presentation and will be in a better position to diagnose learning blocks when they occur. Since this activity is aimed at ascertaining levels of understanding, all answers are right answers.

Activity: Free Association

Level: Grades 1-4

Purpose: To help students become more expressive.

Procedure: The teacher says a word, and the student responds by saying the first word that comes to his or her mind. The student is then asked to explain why he or she associated that particular word with the stimulus word. There are many variations of this activity. One, aimed at vocabulary development, asks the student to say a word that is the opposite of the stimulus word. Another has the child think of a stimulus word and also try to guess the responses that the other children will make to that word. Still another variation uses stimulus and response sentences and phrases instead of words—for example, "If you get flour, salt, sugar, eggs, and a mixing bowl, you are about to . . . (bake a cake)" (see Farrand & Schamber, 1977).

Activity: Definition Match

Level: Grades 2-6

Purpose: To help students increase their vocabulary.

Procedure: Cut up old dictionaries, separating words from their definitions. Have the student correctly match words and definitions. This activity is especially good for tutorial situations.

Activity: Speech Notebook

Level: Grades 1-3

Purpose: To promote more effective verbal expression in students.

Procedure: When the child verbalizes (as in Show and Tell), he or she is rewarded for the correct use of words and sentences by having them recorded in his or her personal speech notebook. In this activity the behavior-modification technique of "catching the child being good" is used to increase fluency of verbal expression. Avoid putting pressure on the student, since feelings of discomfort disrupt verbal fluency.

Activity: Observation Roll Call

Level: Grades 1-3

Purpose: To promote the students' mastery of syntax and to increase their ability to remember details.

Procedure: When taking an oral roll call, have the students answer by describing in a complete sentence something they saw on the way to school.

Activity: Word for the Day

Level: Grade 1-Adult

Purpose: To increase the students' vocabulary development.

Procedure: Establish a "word bank." Each day the students provide, with your help if necessary, a new word and its definition for the bank. Encourage the students to use the word and reinforce in some manner each appropriate use of the word. The process of "banking" the word is in itself reinforcing to the students.

Activity: Game of WORDS

Level: Grades 1-6

Purpose: To build the students' vocabulary.

Procedure: This activity is a modification of bingo and uses pictures and words instead of numbers. To play the game, you need WORDS cards. These are cards divided into 25 squares (see Figure 6-4). Put in each of the 5

W	O	R	D	S
WATCH	ONE	RULER	DOG	SNOW
WORLD	OVEN	RAZOR	DOOR	SPEAR
WATER	OCTOPUS	FREE SPACE	DOCTOR	SNAKE
WAFFLE	OX	ROBE	DOLL	SUIT-CASE
WORM	OWL	RABBIT	DEER	SHOE

Figure 6-4. WORDS card.

squares of each vertical column a word beginning with the letter *W, O, R, D,* or *S.* (The words should, of course, vary from card to card.) From a box or other container, randomly pick pictures naming or illustrating the words that appear on the cards. Announce them as you would in a bingo game. The children look at the picture you have picked and decide whether any of the words on their cards matches the picture. If it does, they cover the space with a token (or a paper clip, or other marker). As in bingo, the first student to complete a line diagonally, horizontally, or vertically is the winner and becomes the next caller. A variation of this activity utilizes definitions and words instead of pictures and words.

Activity: Opposites, or Tell Me Something Different

Level: Grades 1-3

Purpose: To have the students practice the conceptualization and verbal expression of opposites.

Procedure: Present a word and then use it in a sentence. Have the student use a word of opposite meaning in the same skeletal sentence. For example, you say "*Slow.* I saw a slow turtle," and the student replies "I saw a fast turtle."

As a variation of this game, make flash cards of words. Read the word to the student; if the student can tell an opposite of that word, he or she gets to keep the card until the end of the lesson. The same activity can be done in small groups, with the first student to come up with an opposite keeping the card until the end of the game.

Activity: Sentence Completion

Level: Grade 1

Purpose: To encourage the students to use effective verbal expressions and correct syntax.

Procedure: Begin a sentence describing something or expressing action and have the students finish the sentence—for example, "A horse . . . (is big; has four legs; has a tail; can be ridden; and so on)" or "A horse . . . (runs, gallops, trots, walks, and so on)."

As a variation, use riddles or provide a description or definition and have the student supply the correct answers—for example, "Something that is big, has a trunk and a tail, and eats peanuts in the circus . . . (is an elephant)."

Activity: Vocabulary Ball

Level: Grades 1-6

Purpose: To encourage the students to use more extensive vocabulary.

Procedure: Seat the students in a large circle and give a large ball to one of them. Have the child ask a question involving words and slowly roll the ball toward another student. When the ball reaches the other student, he or she must answer the question. The questions should be formulated in complete sentences—for example, "Stephanie, give me another word for *big*," "Bob, say a word that means something we do with our ears," or "Mary, tell me a word that ends in *ing*." If the child receiving the ball gives the right answer, he or she gets to roll the ball for the next turn; if the child gives the wrong answer or no answer, the ball goes to the child next to him or her. The tempo of the game can be varied according to the group's level by changing the speed at which the children are allowed to roll the ball. In some cases you may have to designate a word category before the game starts.

A variation of this game is to choose a category and play "Spin the Bottle," with the student toward whom the bottle points having to say the right word. Instead of using a bottle, you can make a simple pointer device, which can be spun with a flick of the finger (see Farrand & Schamber, 1977).

Activity: Constructing Learning Centers

Level: Grades 1-8

Purpose: To help teachers set up learning centers for classroom and hall displays.

Procedure: The project counselors assisted teachers and students in collecting references and source materials to set up learning centers. Branan (1972) offers several suggestions for incorporating learning centers into the school program. The following suggestions and sources for stocking learning centers come from Branan's article and from the teachers and the counselors in the project centers.

Math Center

Poker chips, abacus, rulers, yardsticks, tape measures, string, rope, homemade number lines, balance beams, scales, objects for counting, sorting, and weighing (buttons, marbles, sugar cubes, washers, poker chips, cereal, acorns, and geoboards), attribute blocks, building blocks, 14 x 2 board with seven nails and painted washers (a device for learning place value), clocks, stopwatch, cash register, play money, homemade and commercial games (such as checkers and chess), graph paper, scrap paper, ads and articles using numbers, Lego blocks, dominoes, workbooks, assignment sheets and job cards, books about math, puzzles, playing cards, interlocking shapes, bead frame, combination locks.

Science Center

Water and sand trays, bottles, cans, pails, funnels, pitchers, scoops, sieves, sifters, basters, straws, spoons, sponges, beakers, prisms, lenses, microscopes, magnifying glasses, mirrors, magnets, bottletops, coins, screws, old motors, radios, gears, candles, flashlights, bulbs, batteries, magnetic compass, electromagnet, electric bells, pendulum, binoculars, telescope, sundial, homemade incubator, small animals, fish, insects, plants, terrarium, aquarium, seeds, eggs, books about science and scientists, dissecting tools, cardboard, poster board, pulleys, weights, rubber tubing, alcohol burners.

Arts and Crafts Center

Paints, paper, clay, easels, brushes, string, foil, fabric, Styrofoam, balsa wood, knives, paste, masking tape, staplers, wallpaper sample books, sewing materials, tools, old railroad ties, shoe boxes, tubes, pie plates, coffee cans, egg crates, pipe cleaners, rubber bands, paper clips, corks, play dough, magazines.

Drama Center

Platform (one table turned on its side on top of another works well), old clothes, props, puppet theater (the empty shell of an old TV set can do the job), puppets (old socks make great hand puppets), materials for making puppets, masks, paper bags, cassette tape recorders, videotape equipment if possible.

Language Arts Center

Single copies of textbooks, paperbacks, library books, encyclopedias, magazines, newspapers, comic books, maps, catalogs, wanted posters, street signs, directions on how to build things, handbills, campaign literature, *Reader's Digest* "Skill Builders," phone books, student-written books, recorders, record players, tapes, records, filmstrips, films, acetate pencils, transparencies, overhead projector, paper, pens, Magic Markers, crayons, camera, typewriter, photographs, flash cards, telephones, word games, crossword puzzles, linguistic blocks, sandpaper letters, magnetic ABC board.

Activity: Working with the School Psychologist

Level: Grades 1-12

Purpose: To coordinate student/personnel services.

Procedure: Several project counselors worked closely with a school psychologist or psychological consultant. During the last year of the Title III Project, the State Department of Education placed considerable emphasis on the need to identify students with special learning needs. The school counselors found that they could perform a number of important functions to ensure that adequate and complete evaluations would be conducted. The counselors didn't do the psychological evaluations themselves but took the following steps before the psychologist tested the students:

1. The school counselor and the principal set up some kind of procedure to "screen" the potential problem students from the student body. (Such procedure involved obtaining teacher recommendations and/or conducting some kind of group standardized testing.)
2. Once a list of pupils to be evaluated had been developed, the school counselor

   a. assisted the teacher in completing a referral sheet,
   b. observed the students in a variety of settings and recorded observations,
   c. checked cumulative records for completeness,
   d. obtained any needed data such as sociograms,
   e. informed parents of plans for referral and obtained their consent,
   f. compared present problems with actions previously taken, methods formerly used, and areas successfully explored in the past,
   g. arranged physical examinations when needed.

   When the psychologist was actually present in the school, the counselor found it helpful to introduce the children to him or her. The counselor was also available for conferences with the evaluator and arranged several meetings among teachers, parents, principal, children, and evaluator.
   After the psychologist left the school, the counselor performed a number of follow-up functions such as:

1. Assisting the teacher in implementing the psychologist's suggestions,

2. Continuing to monitor the students' progress,
3. Providing feedback and follow-up to the evaluator.

It has been estimated that it takes a school psychologist at least 12 hours to gather the data necessary to formulate an educational plan for each of the referred students. By taking the steps mentioned above, the project counselors were able to decrease this amount of time considerably and actually increase the quality of the evaluation and plan.

Activity: Classroom Discussion on Learning Disabilities

Level: Grades 3-8, teachers, and parents

Purpose: To create empathy and understanding for students with learning disabilities; to increase teacher and parent awareness of students' learning disabilities.

Procedure:

1. Ask the participants to write their full names on 3 x 5 cards while holding the cards to their foreheads.
2. Invite the participants to evaluate the quality of their writing according to the accepted standards of neatness and accuracy.
3. Give the group members the opportunity to express the feelings they had during the activity.
4. Point out that many students with learning disabilities face handicaps similar to those experienced by the participants during the exercise every time they attempt to complete homework assignments.
5. Point out that wearing glasses or contact lenses and having poor coordination may often be classified as types of learning disabilities.
6. Show the filmstrip *A Walk in Another Pair of Shoes* and discuss Dean's situation and how his classmates should respond to him.
7. Discuss with teacher and parent groups the following ways of recognizing children with learning disabilities in grades 1 through 8:
   a. Does your child or student show signs of hyperactivity? Hyperactivity is defined as an above-normal activity level. Sometimes the child may behave like a caged lion—always pacing and on the move. This excessive physical movement is often accompanied by an unusually high rate of talking (motormouth). Remember, though, that most children have their periods of hyperactivity.
   b. Does your child or student have above-average coordination problems? Does he or she often run into things and have trouble

playing sports involving throwing, catching, kicking, and hitting a ball? Does the child have difficulty staying within the lines when coloring or tracing picture mazes with a pencil? Frequently these symptoms point to problems with size and depth perception (the child will see things as being larger or smaller than they really are).

c. Does your child or student get distracted easily? Many children who suffer from learning disabilities have difficulty shutting out background noises, thereby finding it extremely difficult to hear the teacher's directions. Other attention disorders include short attention span and the tendency to tune the world out. In short, these disorders make it difficult for the child to pay attention to detail. During a spelling test, the child may not even hear four or five words in a row.

d. Does your child or student have comprehension problems? Frequently, because of comprehension problems, the child sees little, if any, relationship among items, events, and facts. Sometimes children who seem to articulate well when speaking have difficulty understanding or explaining what they read.

e. Does your child or student have a left- or right-dominance problem? A typical learning-disability symptom is general confusion between left and right. For example, some children write or throw a ball with both the left and the right hand—generally with equally poor results.

f. Does your child or student perform inconsistently from one day to the next? There seems to be a "leaky-bucket syndrome" operating in some children with learning disabilities. Information learned one day may not be there the next day. The best way to deal with this problem is to impart learning in small steps that are highly meaningful to the child's life. (Of course, this is a desirable teaching strategy with all children.)

g. Does your child or student have adjustment problems? Children with learning disabilities find it extremely frustrating—more, perhaps, than other children—when they realize that they have trouble doing what everybody else seems to be handling easily. Self-concept suffers, and, with older children, failure often leads to delinquent behavior. Many children with learning disabilities exhibit extreme mood swings—happy and cooperative one moment, sullen or aggressive the next. When these students' classmates, teachers, and family ridicule them or put them down, all of their problems, especially adjustment problems, become more acute.

h. Does your child or student act impulsively? Sometimes children with learning disabilities seem to act and react before thinking, without allowing time for evaluating the feedback they get from their behavior and from the reactions of others. This impulsiveness may indicate that they are not aware of the consequences of their behavior.

i. Does your child or student have orientation problems? Children with learning disabilities often seem confused and mixed up. They may forget the time of day or even the day of the week.

j. Does your child or student seem less mature than other children of the same age? Many children with learning disabilities exhibit immature behavior because their social learning is impeded by the same factors that slow down their academic progress. Defective speech may also accompany some learning disabilities, especially those concerning auditory perception.

8. Discuss what parents and teachers can do to help children with learning disabilities.

   a. Check for physical problems that may not be related to learning disabilities. See a good pediatrician who has experience with learning disabilities.

   b. If your pediatrician confirms that your student or child has a learning disability, request an evaluation from your school system's evaluation team. The same evaluation could be done in a community hospital or diagnostic center.

   c. Make sure that your school can provide an individualized program that meets the recommendations of the evaluation team or diagnostic center.

Resource:

A Walk in Another Pair of Shoes, a filmstrip distributed by CANMC (P.O. Box 604 Main Office, Los Angeles, Calif. 90053).

Chapter Seven

CAREER DEVELOPMENT

Another primary area of focus in the school guidance program is career education. Students in the elementary grades need help in obtaining relevant information about careers and vocations. Experts agree that awareness of one's abilities and interests as they relate to future employment should begin in elementary school. Once such awareness has been developed, the student is ready to explore occupations or job clusters. Career education also means learning to plan and make decisions. In sum, career development is a continuous process of exploration that, when successful, leads to vocational adjustment and fulfillment. One way of ensuring such success is to begin the process early.

The rationale for including career education in the school guidance program is based on the following points:

1. Career education is historically a part of school guidance programs.
2. Career education is regarded by both parents and teachers as an integral part of school guidance.
3. Career-education materials and resources are readily available to school guidance programs.
4. Career education is an essential component of a relevant curriculum.
5. Career education should be centered in the classroom and integrated in the regular school curriculum.

School counselors have a number of functions relating to their overall involvement in career education. Counselors can promote career study through orientation and public-relations activities. They also act as resource persons for those teachers who relate their subject areas to career education and skill development. Also, school counselors can conduct surveys of community resources for career study and assist teachers in career-educational planning, follow-up activities, and program evaluation. In essence, school counselors serve as instigators and coordinators of career education in the schools.

Many career and educational plans can be discussed in small-group sessions.

The following activities are considered very effective tools for the school counselor involved in career guidance. The activities are presented with sufficient details to be implemented as a part of an overall program of career education. We said "a part" because the activities should *not* be considered to be a complete career-education program in themselves. Rather, they are activities intended to enrich the career curriculum and thereby make it more viable and relevant to the student. Instruments 15-18 in Appendix C are evaluative tools that teacher and counselor can use to determine whether the career-education objectives have been met.

A few general suggestions apply to the implementation of any career-education programs. Here they are:

1. Use as many resource people and occupational-role models as possible.
2. Have the parents participate in a variety of ways—assisting in planning field trips; sharing information about their jobs, travel, and hobbies; and making suggestions about the program.
3. Use drama and role playing to help students experience as many of the affective aspects of job roles as possible.

Activity: Hobby Days

Level: Grades 4-12

Purpose: To have students share their hobbies as a means of discovering vocational interests related to such hobbies.

Procedure: Have the students plan a Hobby Fair or Hobby Seminar, in which classmates display the products of their various hobbies. Have the class investigate the occupations that are related to particular hobbies. People who are seriously involved in a hobby may be invited to visit the class to "kick off" hobby study by discussing their own hobbies with the students. This activity can be as big or as small as the school or class wants to make it. Some schools may want to celebrate a Hobby Week or have an Interest Fair. Any such celebration, however, should represent the culminating activity of a period of exploration of interests on the part of the students. Without such explorations, the celebration would have little value.

The teacher may also want to invite the students to choose a new hobby and write a description of it that includes practical aspects such as how much it costs. Another possibility is to set up a hobby corner in which students display the products of their hobbies throughout the year.

Activity: Finding Activities Related to Careers in the School Setting

Level: Grades 4-12

Purpose: To identify and utilize all vocational resources within the school.

Procedure: Running a school requires the performance of many specialized functions on the part of many specialized people. Often the same person performs a variety of activities. For example, the school principal functions as an accountant and as a personnel director, not to mention his or her many other roles. The students can carry out a full-scale investigation of all these functions and roles.

School clubs and extracurricular activities can also help students learn about occupations. One approach is to have students interview organizational officers in order to determine their functions and then think of careers that require similar functions. Students like the idea of searching the school for career information. And the organizational officers like to describe the variety of skills required to do their jobs.

Activity: Career Hats

Level: Grades 1-3

Purpose: To have the children identify the uniforms (especially the headgear) associated with various occupations.

Materials: Various headgear associated with different occupations.

Procedure: Assemble a variety of the actual headgear used by various occupational groups. Have the students consider and discuss why different "hats" are required for different occupations. In the course of the discussion someone is likely to bring up the elements of safety and hygiene, which are the main reasons for wearing certain outfits and headgear in certain types of occupations. Have the students focus on this important aspect of career education and encourage them to use drama and role playing to enliven the discussion about occupational settings, their dangers, and safety measures.

Most children enjoy wearing different headgear and identifying the wide variety of hats they notice on workers in the community. If feasible, ask resource people to visit the class and bring along equipment and paraphernalia related to their occupations. One of the project counselors invited a carpenter, who brought his tools, demonstrated them in class, and encouraged the students to name some of the tools and describe their uses.

Activity: Ring Toss

Level: Grade 1-Adult

Purpose: To help students become aware of how competitive they are and discover whether they are motivated by individual or by team interests.

Materials: Pegs, rings, score sheets, and masking tape are needed to mark each foot (1 to 10 feet) from the peg. One point is given for each foot from the peg for each successful toss.

Procedure: The Ring Toss game can be played with many variations. All players can be given a number of practice tosses. After the practice round, the players can compete against each other; high score wins. Another variation may be to form teams to compete against each other. Teams can be balanced on the basis of the scores of the individual round. A handicap round of play might be completed, with low scorers being given handicap points in order to "even up" the contest.

Discussion of each round may focus on what players learned from their successes or failures. Did the players challenge themselves?

Resource:
Motivation Workshops, by D. C. McClelland and R. S. Steele (New York: General Learning Press, 1972).

Activity: Cooperation/Competition Posters

Level: Grade 3-Adult

Purpose: To help students test what they know about a variety of careers and learn more about the value of both cooperation and competition.

Materials: Provide each group of five to six students with one magazine per student, a large piece of poster board, paste or glue, a pair of scissors, and a Magic Marker.

Procedure: Select an occupational theme and ask each group to make a poster illustrating a specific occupation within the chosen theme (for example, if the theme is "health careers," some of the occupations may be surgeon, nurse, lab technician, ambulance driver, and so on). An occupation can be illustrated only once, and the groups may be given a time limit during which to complete the task. The posters are then judged on the basis of technical accuracy, artistic quality, and creativity.

After the competition, all the students may get together to discuss how cooperation within each group made competition among groups possible. All the posters can then be displayed as examples of team work. Also, a member of each group may be asked to describe to the entire class what his or her group's poster illustrates. This activity is a good combination of active participation and discussion and can be adapted to many variations.

Activity: Visitor's Interview

Level: Grade 1-Adult

Purpose: To help students focus on their occupational interests, formulate appropriate questions about jobs and careers, and consider how people make career choices.

Materials: Tape recorder.

Procedure: Invite a person whose occupation is of particular interest to the students to visit the class. Before the resource person's visit, motivate the students by asking "Have you seen or heard television or radio programs in which people are interviewed about their jobs? What types of questions are asked? If you were the interviewer, what would you like to know about someone who is a _____ (carpenter, business executive, bus driver, or whatever the occupation of the resource person is)?" Students may be asked to write down their questions before the scheduled visit and bring them to class. Using a tape recorder, the students interview the visitor about his or her occupation. The tape recording of the interview is then made available at a listening center, so that the students can listen to it after the meeting.

The group interview is even more valuable if the students are allowed to select the person or persons to be interviewed. A variation of this activity is to have a student role-play a person with a particular occupation, highlighting a different occupation each week.

Resources:
"Designing Success Strategies," a television course by William A. Glasser.
Values Clarification, by S. Simon, L. Howe, and H. Kirschenbaum (New York: Hart, 1972).

Activity: Career Jeopardy

Level: Grades 4-12

Purpose: To learn about the jobs performed by various workers; the equipment, tools, and machinery they use; and how one works as a member of a team.

Materials: Lumber, nails, cardboard, and Magic Markers.

Procedure: Build a Jeopardy board large enough for all players to read it easily. The board should have five columns with five slots in each column. Two strips of tagboard are placed in each slot. One piece of tagboard shows an answer; the other, which is placed over it, shows the amount the player or team receives for giving the correct question to the answer. Jeopardy is a game that reverses the normal question-answer order by showing the player an answer and asking him or her to supply the question relating to that answer. For example, the player is shown the answer "A term used to describe a man who drives a bulldozer" and asked to provide the correct question, which is "What is a catskinner?" Numerous answer/question pairs are needed before play can begin. Five or six answer/question pairs should be developed for each career category. The same categories may be used frequently; however, five new answer/question pairs should be developed each time a category is used.

For the rules of play, the teacher or counselor is referred to the Jeopardy game's directions. Jeopardy is available for purchase at most bookstores and department stores. Some of the students in the class are likely to either own the game or know where to get it. Having the original game available is very helpful when building the Career Jeopardy set and when learning to play the game.

One extremely valuable variation of Career Jeopardy is the use of team play. Students who are not functioning as scorekeeper, timekeeper, announcer, or operator of the Career Jeopardy board are divided into three teams, and a spokesperson is selected to state the question the team thinks belongs to the answer displayed on the Career Jeopardy board.

Resource:
Jeopardy game (commercially available).

Activity: Career Bingo

Level: Grades 5-6

Purpose: To help students become familiar with various occupations.

Materials: King Features commercial kit and markers.

Procedure: Count off by 4s. Have each group of four form a circle. Give each student a Career Bingo card and a small supply of markers (beans, paper clips, or pebbles, for example). Call out a description of a job and have students identify the job aloud. (After the initial game, don't repeat answers that have already been given. Instead, let those students who remember the answer cover the appropriate square.)

Resource:
King Features commercial kit (King Features, 235 E. 45th St., New York, N.Y. 10017).

Activity: Community Visits or Field Trips

Level: Grade 3-Adult

Purpose: To help students become interested in career opportunities.

Procedure: The community visit or field trip offers students an opportunity to be directly involved in activities related to various career opportunities. When effectively used as a part of career education, it also offers the school counselor a good opportunity to demonstrate to the teachers the value of field trips.

Field trips can be effective and stimulating, but they can also be useless and dull. It is therefore important to identify those factors that make a field trip valuable not only to the class but also to the teacher's professional development. Members of the ESEA Title III Project have been able to develop a format for what may be called a nontraditional field trip or community visit.

The format is simple in design but requires hard work and careful planning to ensure full value. The first step is to develop student and teacher involvement. The counselor may start by conducting a classroom group meeting to determine what the students already know about career opportunities within their community. The discussion can begin by defining various terms, such as *career, work, occupation, employment, industry,* and *business.* If the meeting is successful, the participants will want to learn more about the terms discussed. The meeting may also be the springboard for various career-related activities. For example, the students may decide to treat their trip to and from school as an "expedition" offering countless opportunities for discovery. At an appointed time, the students/explorers will report to their classmates about their discoveries—that is, the interesting kinds of occupations and works they noticed on their expeditions. The role of reporter may be added to that of explorer and notes taken. The students may be interested in comparing the types of workers they see in the morning with those they see in the afternoon. As a matter of fact, they may become so interested in the various patterns of work that they may decide to extend their explorations to other times such as weekends and evenings.

The next step in the format is the actual planning of the visit. Students, teacher, and counselor are all involved in deciding what the best places to visit would be. Should the class visit familiar places and attempt to find out more about them? Or should they, instead, visit unfamiliar places? Should the class visit as a group, or should only a few students make the visit and report to the rest of the class about the trip? If so, who is going to go? Are they going to take pictures and use videotapes?

The planning involves much more. The students make decisions about the rules necessary for field trips and, if at all possible, actually make the phone calls and write the letters to arrange the field trip. The students may even need to raise the money necessary for the field trip. The project counselors reported that the most successful community visits were those that used volunteers (parents or friends) to drive students on the field trips. The use of volunteers not only cuts the costs of community visits but also provides additional adults to supervise the students.

After the planning is done and the procedures and rules for the visits established, the students get busy with various activities that should precede the actual trip. They determine what things to look for and develop the necessary techniques to ensure that they will obtain the information

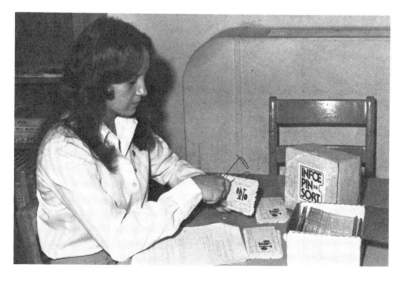

Effective guidance programs offer a variety of resource materials in career education.

they want. At one project school, the students prepared interview questions for the persons they expected to encounter during their visits. The students also role-played the interviews before their visits. A number of forms can be used to help students remember what they are to do during the visit.

The next step in the format is the interaction itself — that is, the interaction between the students and the people being visited. Students are encouraged to find out as much as they can not only about the occupations in question but also about the people and how they feel about their work. The interaction phase of the community-visit format stresses the importance of the students' bringing back to class the "feeling" or atmosphere of the place they visited. This means interacting enough with the workers they visit to be able to tell, for example, whether they are happy or disgruntled.

The final phase of the community visit consists of the follow-up and evaluation. Students are asked to share their experience by preparing "I learned that _____" statements, to offer suggestions for improvement, and to discuss the visit with their parents and friends. Scrapbooks or displays about the field trips are useful ways of re-creating and maintaining the feelings they had about the visit.

The value of the community visit and of the format suggested above is substantiated by the proven effectiveness of the career-awareness activities carried out by the project. The results of the three years of project activities demonstrate that the units dealing with career guidance were the most consistent in goal attainment. The community visit, together with the classroom visit, is a vital segment of a career-guidance program. In other words, the community visit is one technique that can demonstrate quickly and clearly the impact of the guidance program on students, teachers, and parents.

Field trips as a part of the career-guidance program also help teachers see how field trips may be used to promote learning in other curricula. Also, by observing the procedures used by the elementary school counselor, teachers can learn how to plan community visits appropriately and efficiently. But even if the teachers do not utilize field trips in other curricula, the students still benefit directly from the visits outside the walls of the school building.

Activity: Simulated Proposal for Career Education

Level: Intermediate grades-Adult

Purpose: To stimulate teacher and parent interest in a program of career development.

Procedure: Divide the students into small groups of four to six members. Ask the participants to write a proposal for career development, as if they were a guidance committee, based on the following hypothetical situation.

You are a school counselor, teacher, or administrator serving on the guidance committee for this school year. *Your school is in a rural area, and most of the children are from low and middle socioeconomic environments.* (Change the portion in italics to fit your situation. The level of the hypothetical school is up to you or your group to decide. It may be elementary, junior high, senior high, or college.)

Federal funds are available to those who write and submit a suitable proposal for career development. The proposal must deal with the specific projects, materials, and programs that you intend to implement in your school.

You originally had over a month to write your proposal. However, because of a clerical error, you have just been informed that the deadline for the proposal is noon today. (Your supervisor has called the guidance committee together and explained the situation a little while ago.) Since it is now 11 o'clock, you have less than an hour in which to write your proposal. In fact, since you will have to type it and deliver it to the Board of Education, you have only 30 minutes.

Obviously, you won't be able to write a book in 30 minutes. It is, therefore, better if you spend 10 minutes brainstorming and 20 minutes writing two or three main ideas for the proposal. Remember that this proposal deals with action plans and programs, not just with theoretical justifications.

Chapter Eight

COUNSELING AND GUIDANCE TECHNIQUES FOR CLASSROOM DISCIPLINE

According to several recent Gallup Poll surveys and similar reports by the American Personnel and Guidance Association, discipline is ranked by teachers as their number-one problem. Violence, vandalism, and other forms of lack of discipline are the greatest concern of teachers throughout the country. Few teachers were surprised to learn that the Senate Subcommittee to Investigate Juvenile Delinquency found that the primary objective of public schooling is no longer education but preservation. The same subcommittee reported in 1977 that public schools are currently spending $600 million each year to repair the damage caused by vandalism. The $600-million figure approaches the total textbook cost for one year and would be sufficient to employ an additional 50,000 teachers without increasing taxes! Furthermore, serious physical assaults on teachers and other individuals in our schools have risen by 58% over the last five years, with sex offenses increasing by 62%, drug-related crimes by 81%, and robberies by 117%.

The Senate subcommittee was long on documentation of the school discipline problem but, unfortunately, short on solutions. The subcommittee is not alone. If effective methods for managing discipline were practiced on a large scale, the results would be reflected in the data. The need to develop new discipline practices in the school seems obvious. The present methods are not working! The purpose of this chapter is to present guidance and counseling methods for managing classroom discipline.

These methods have been researched and have proven to be effective 80 to 95% of the time. Needless to say, if one technique worked all the time with all the students, the task of implementing new disciplinary approaches in the schools would be much simpler. But the fact is that not only do different students require different approaches but each student may require a different approach at different times. So, just as good baseball pitchers need more than one type of pitch to be effective players, good teachers and counselors need more than one type of "pitch" to be effective teachers of discipline.

The "change of pace," or role shift, is a basic approach to the teaching of discipline and requires a number of different techniques on the part of teachers and counselors. It works by disturbing an established routine, thus jolting the parties out of ineffective behavior. When communication between student and teacher has deteriorated beyond a certain point, a change of pace by one of the parties frequently results in improved behavior in the other one. For example, if a teacher who has responded only to a student's misbehavior chooses, instead, to "catch" the student in good behavior, it is likely that the student will engage in good behavior more and more frequently. Similarly, if a student who normally tries to attract attention through misbehavior decides, instead, to gain attention by completing at least one assignment per day, it is likely that the teacher will start to pay more attention to the student's accomplishments. In both cases,

Counselor-teacher consultation is helpful in determining how to teach discipline to students.

the change of pace on the part of one person will result in a change of pace on the part of the other, because everyone's timing has been disturbed to the point that the old, ineffective roles cannot be reenacted.

The following four role-shift strategies for teaching discipline to students represent practical applications of the above principles:

1. Using logical consequences in conjunction with the four goals of misbehavior.
2. Using classroom meetings for problem solving.
3. Using a counseling-and-contract approach based on reality therapy.
4. Using an individualized ten-step lesson plan for teaching discipline.

USING LOGICAL CONSEQUENCES IN CONJUNCTION WITH THE FOUR GOALS OF MISBEHAVIOR

As we mentioned in Chapter Four, practitioners of Individual Psychology (see Dreikurs, 1968) see misbehavior as an attempt to achieve one or more of the following four goals: (1) attention, (2) power, (3) revenge, and (4) display of inadequacy. Generally these goals of misbehavior are the result of a failure to achieve feelings of self-worth or of lack of loving concern from significant people. For example, if you cannot get positive attention from someone, it is likely that you will seek negative attention rather than be ignored. Consequently, in order to be noticed, you will resort to one of your attention-getting misbehaviors.

What is the best way to deal with someone who appears to pursue one of the four goals of misbehavior? We (the authors) support the approach called *logical consequences* over those interventions commonly classified as punishment. The logical-consequences approach stresses the natural, common-sense outcomes of misbehavior, whereas punishment techniques often have no relationship to the misbehavior. For example, if Linda is 20 minutes late for dinner, one assumes that she is not hungry, and her plate is removed. If she wants dinner, she must fix it herself. This is the logical-consequences approach. The punishment approach, instead, would call for lectures on responsibility, no TV for a day or more, and, quite likely, diatribes on Linda's shortcomings, almost completely unrelated to her being late for dinner. All of these punishing techniques have an attention-getting payoff, even if the attention is a negative one.

Disruptive classroom behavior is best treated logically by removing the offender from the group so that he or she is not allowed to infringe on the right of other students to learn. Paddlings can no longer be considered logical consequences of disruptive behavior, since their counterparts in life outside the school building—floggings and the whipping pillory—are no longer accepted forms of punishment in our society. Furthermore, paddlings have proven to be singularly ineffective with most students. We shall return to these points later in our discussion. In sum, the main reasons for our advocacy of logical consequences as intervention methods are that (1) they help establish good relationships between adults and students by teaching acceptance of responsibility for the outcome of one's own behavior and (2) they expose the child to the reality of the social order.

How is the concept of logical consequences applied to each of the four goals of misbehavior? The first step is to identify which goal or goals the student is trying to achieve through misbehavior. Awareness of what you, the teacher, are feeling is often the best clue for identifying the goal of the student's misbehavior. The following chart tells you how you are likely to feel when you confront each of the four goals of misbehavior.

You feel:	*When the goal is:*
annoyed	attention
threatened	power
hurt	revenge
helpless	display of inadequacy

For example, your feeling annoyed is likely to be the result of the student's attention-getting behavior. You won't feel threatened by attention-seeking behavior—at least not until the student's repeated attempts to gain attention and your efforts to ignore them evolve into a power struggle. When that happens, you will feel threatened because your authority, power, or place is being challenged. If, instead, you feel hurt, you are probably responding to the child's need for revenge. A feeling of helplessness generally accompanies one's unsuccessful efforts to help others improve, especially when they display inadequacy. So, by being in touch with your own feelings, you can identify the goals of your students' misbehaviors.

Each goal carries a message that we think is important for the adult to hear and reflect to the child. Generally this reflection, expressed as a guess, should take place when the relationship is not under stress or in crisis. In other words, wait until the discipline situation has cooled down and then talk with the student about the goal of his or her behavior. For example:

"Could it be that you want me to pay more attention to you than I have done in the past?" is a good way to reflect the student's attempt to gain attention.

"Could it be that you want to be the boss and make more decisions and choices on your own?" is a good way to guess about power seeking.

"Could it be that someone has hurt you and you want to hurt someone in return?" is a statement that reflects the revenge motive. "Could it be that you want me to get off your back, and the only way you know how to do it is to do poor work?" tells the student that you suspect a display of inadequacy.

These "could it be" questions can be followed up with regular counseling interviews focusing on various alternatives for helping students achieve their goals.

Specific interventions or procedures can be designed to prevent the child's misbehavior strategies from succeeding. The following are a few examples of interventions that focus on logical consequences rather than on punishment.

Goal	Interventions
Attention	Ignore the behavior when possible and catch the student in good behavior. Deprive the student of his or her audience, if necessary by isolating him or her from the rest of the class. At the same time arrange helpful ways for the student to gain positive attention.
Power	Give the student a choice between two or more acceptable alternatives. Use grade and behavior contracts that reward the student with free time or in some other manner when work is completed. Don't become involved in hostile confrontations. Let the student have a voice in determining and changing class rules.
Revenge	Stop punishment or punitive methods. If you are unable to achieve a positive interaction with the student, find him or her a friend. Assist the student in devising helpful plans for handling anger.
Display of inadequacy	Don't exert any kind of pressure. Stop grading for a while. Find the student's achievement level. Use large doses of encouragement. Ensure success experiences every day.

Note that several of the activities presented in the first part of Chapter Four (through "Tattling") can be used to teach the subject of discipline.

USING CLASSROOM MEETINGS FOR PROBLEM SOLVING

Classroom meetings to solve social problems provide an excellent format for working with the class on discipline problems. These meetings can be used to establish or change the class rules and to resolve difficulties when the rules are broken. The general guidelines for leading classroom meetings were presented in Chapter Two ("Group Approaches for Building Self-Esteem").

We have found that classrooms with well-defined rules work better than those without stated rules. Classrooms also work better when the rules are established with the students' cooperation and are based on agreement. Students and teachers can use classroom meetings to discuss the need to change those rules that are not working well. The consequences for breaking each rule should be clearly spelled out during the meetings to avoid confusion and misunderstanding. Perhaps the most significant aspect of good classroom meetings is that they help students feel good about being in a classroom in which their voices are heard. It is doubtful that any discipline program will be effective in a bad school or bad classroom. How can we teach students to be responsible and respectful in a classroom or school that has no meaning in their lives or where teachers demonstrate their own irresponsibility by using ineffective discipline approaches over and over again?

The rules and rule-breaking consequences established in the classroom meetings can be posted on the bulletin board as a reminder to all class members. Short and specific rule lists are the most effective. Teachers and counselors are often surprised to discover how well most student groups can handle the rule-making assignment, without heavy-handed supervision by those in charge. When a rule is broken, the teacher can call time-out and announce "You are breaking *our* rule!"

The following is an outline of a problem-solving classroom meeting focusing on setting rules.

Identify the topic:
The question for our first classroom meeting is "What rules do we need to have in our classroom this year?"
Ask for definitions:
What do we mean when we talk about classroom rules?
Personalize the discussion and ask for specifics:
What classroom rules have you had in other classes?
What rules do you have at home?
Can you think of other places in which you have or had to observe rules?
Ask for value judgments and agreements/disagreements:
Why do we have rules?
What are some good rules? Why?
What are some bad rules? Why?

Classroom meetings can be effectively used to work on discipline problems.

What rules would you like to have for our class?
Do you know someone who would agree with you about the rules you'd like
for our class? Who?
Do you know someone who would probably disagree with you about the rules
you like? Why?
How many of us should agree on a rule before we make it a classroom rule?
Challenge the group:
What rules would you be willing to follow in our class?
What should we do if our rules are broken?
What should we do if someone makes it hard for you to learn or hard for me to
teach?
In what specific ways do some students bother others in the classroom?
What should we do when this happens?
Would two people volunteer to list our rules on the bulletin board?

The Level-1 Contract presented in Chapter Six is a typical example of
what can be achieved during a classroom meeting on rules.

USING REALITY THERAPY AS A COUNSELING
APPROACH FOR DISCIPLINE PROBLEMS

Glasser's (1965) reality-therapy philosophy was discussed in detail in
Chapter Two, in the section on "Individual Approaches for Building Self-

Esteem." Such philosophy, as reflected in the following five basic questions, can be successfully applied by teachers and counselors to situations involving discipline problems. The questions (directed to the misbehaving student) are:

1. What are you doing?
2. How is your behavior helping you?
3. If what you're doing is not helping you, what are some things you could do, instead, that would help you?
4. Which of these things are you going to do?
5. When will you start?

Teachers, principals, and counselors are encouraged to modify the five-question format to fit their individual personality and needs and those of their students. However, all successful modifications usually omit the "why" trap. "Why" questions focus the counseling on excuses for behavior rather than on responsibility for behavior. "Why" questions are best reserved for academic discussions and classroom meetings in which causal thinking is desired. The emphasis in the reality-counseling process is on making a plan for engaging in helpful behavior and then committing oneself to that plan. Developing the will to make a commitment is particularly important to those who have difficulty in completing activities. Frequently these "noncommitters" also pose discipline problems for the teacher. As is the case with most behavior-problem students, the noncommitters often lack the success identity experienced by those students who feel worthwhile and loved. Therefore, we can't overstress the importance of making these students feel that you care enough to help them experience success.

The following interview is one example of the reality-counseling process.

Counselor: Jim. suppose you start by telling me what's going on.
Jim: Well, I was arrested for using dope. I'm really afraid that they're going to kick me out of school for this.
Counselor: OK, so you've been using drugs. I'm wondering how you see this as helping you.
Jim: Before I began using drugs, I wasn't popular, especially with girls. Now that I'm into it, I find that I'm accepted—maybe by just a few people, but that's enough to make me feel good about it.
Counselor: So using drugs does help you make friends, which up to now you haven't been able to do. We might want to take a look at what else you get from drugs.
Jim: Security, maybe.
Counselor: What do you mean by security?
Jim: Well, at home I feel really inferior—always getting put down, you know?

When I can escape from that situation, I feel as if I am making it on my own without anybody's help. I feel like an individual, not just a kid.

Counselor: So taking drugs helps you turn off the pain and helps you *get away* from your troubles. But how is taking drugs helping you solve your problems?

Jim: It makes me feel good about myself.

Counselor: How does taking drugs help you solve your problems?

Jim: You feel good about yourself—right? You're successful, happy, and all that. Confidence—that's what I'm talking about. I need to feel as if what I do is helping me. Since I've gotten into drugs—which, by the way, is only an occasional weekend thing—I know that there are people who care about me. That's why I'm here. I've heard that you care and that you can help me stay out of trouble with the school.

Counselor: How would you like to have me help you stay out of trouble?

Jim: Talk to the principal. I think he knows. Or maybe you could just find out what they'll do to me. My parents were mad enough when I was arrested; they'll die if I'm kicked out of school. Maybe talking to you will help.

Counselor: Well, I *can* guarantee that I will talk with you and listen to you. What are some things you'd like to hear from me?

Jim: That I'm OK. That this trouble is gone. I've got to be honest: I'm still doing drugs. But I don't want you to condemn me for that.

Counselor: How would it help for me to condemn you?

Jim: It wouldn't.

Counselor: I agree. I also won't be able to do any judging for you, either good or bad. It would help me, though, if you would summarize the good and the bad parts of your taking drugs.

Jim: It's good for me because it helps me feel good and make friends. It's bad because . . . it got me in trouble with the law, my parents, and school. I'm no different than a thousand other people that get busted. I'm just unlucky. There's really nothing wrong.

Counselor: What you seem to be saying is that getting arrested and all the rest is not enough to make you stop taking drugs.

Jim: I'll be more careful—that's all.

Counselor: OK. So what would you like me to do for you other than to say you're OK and lay off the not-OK remarks?

Jim: You can be honest. If you think something is wrong, say so.

Counselor: What could possibly be wrong in your life right now? You've made a decision based on your experience. It would appear that taking drugs pays off for you even if the price is a little steep.

Jim: Do you think drugs are wrong? You sound like you might feel the same way I do—you haven't said anything one way or the other.

Counselor: I don't use them.

Jim: (No comment).

Counselor: Let's get together if you want to talk about making a change sometime. Right now you seem pretty determined about continuing what you're doing.

Jim: You will talk to the principal about not kicking me out of school?

Counselor: What would you have me say to him?

Jim: I see your point: I'm not acting in any way that indicates that it won't happen again. You mean business, huh?

Counselor: Yes, I do. I'm here to help you work out a plan if you'd like to change something to help yourself.

Jim: I don't want to hurt my parents anymore. What can you do to help me that way?

Counselor: We can talk about what you do that hurts your parents and decide if you want to do something else.

Jim: Speaking of talking—that's one thing I haven't done with my parents in a long time. Maybe that would help—I know it sounds corny—maybe they'll understand.

Counselor: All right, so talking with them might be one helpful thing. Can you think of any other things we could also consider?

Jim: Quitting drugs—maybe?

Counselor: OK. So, talking with your parents and stopping drugs would make things better with your parents. Is there anything else you could do?

Jim: That's about it.

Counselor: What will you do before our next talk?

Jim: I'll have to talk with my parents and think of something else I need to change, because I'm not too sure about quitting drugs altogether.

Counselor: OK. Will you have that talk and will you bring along a list of the things you're going to do to our next session?

Jim: Sure.

Counselor: What are some things you want to tell your parents during your talk?

Jim: I want them to know that I care enough about them to stop hurting them and that we are working on some plans to do this.

Counselor: We can discuss how things went for you during our next talk. See you next week?

Jim: Right.

USING A TEN-STEP LESSON PLAN FOR TEACHING DISCIPLINE

Just like many other school subjects, discipline as appropriate social behavior is a subject that many students may have never learned well or at all. Lack of discipline can be as serious a handicap as failure to master any of the basic subjects. In fact, failure to learn discipline often prevents successful learning of even the three R's. Therefore, if discipline has not been learned at home, the teacher may need to give priority to this most basic subject. To that end, we present a ten-step lesson plan for teaching discipline to students. The plan, developed from Glasser (1974), Thompson and Cates (1976), and Thompson and Poppen (1972), includes all the interventions discussed in this chapter. For the purpose of the plan, the interventions have been grouped into three phases, with the ten individual steps arranged in hierarchical fashion. The intent is to use as few steps in the hierarchy as possible. Hopefully the discipline problems will disappear during the first three steps, which constitute the relationship phase. Steps 4 through 6 constitute the counseling phase, and steps 7 through 10 make up the time-out phase. The ten-step plan should be adapted to the needs of each student according to the teacher's evaluation of the student and the setting.

It is recommended that teachers and counselors begin by trying the process with one student who has behavior problems. The question is often raised whether one should begin the plan with the worst discipline problem in the class. Since teaching discipline is often a tedious process, many teachers select moderate discipline problems rather than the toughest cases. This is, of course, the teacher's decision. However, it should be kept in mind that the plan has been found to be highly effective even with the most difficult discipline cases.

The Relationship Phase

The relationship phase includes three steps, which are directed toward building a trusting and friendly relationship between student and teacher. Such a relationship is the keystone of the process. Without it, the

A trusting and friendly relationship between student and teacher (or counselor) is the keystone of the relationship phase.

process would ignore one of the two basic human needs that must be met if a person is to achieve a success identity—the need to feel that someone cares. The second need is the need to feel useful and worthwhile. The relationship is established not only by encouraging teachers, counselors, and parents to become more involved with their young people but also by encouraging the students to increase their interaction with others. The relationship phase is generally the most significant part of the ten-step program. The greatest gains in helpful behavior occur consistently during this phase.

Step 1

In Step 1, teachers are invited to become their own reality therapists by asking themselves "What am I doing to correct the behavior of my worst discipline case? How helpful is what I'm doing?" Teachers are asked to list everything they have tried that has not worked and to commit themselves never to engage in these ineffective interventions again. The list can be laminated and taped to the teacher's desk, thus becoming a contract to refrain from doing unhelpful things with the student in question. Of course, these lists often contain many interventions that can be helpful with other students and that, therefore, should not be discarded.

If consultation with the teacher is taking place, it is better if the consultant refrains from offering a plan until the teacher has completely exhausted his or her supply of ideas. The ten-step approach involves a joint effort by consultant and teacher, with the teacher "owning" not only the ideas to be tried but the manner in which the plan will be implemented.

Step 2

Step 2 is the role-shift, or change-of-pace, strategy. As mentioned earlier, the most effective baseball pitchers have a change-of-pace pitch that breaks the hitter's rhythm and timing. Similarly, the effective counselor or teacher tries to break up the student's undesirable behavior patterns. Therefore, it is recommended that the teacher pause for a few seconds after the occurrence of misbehavior to ask the question "What does this student expect me to do?" and then not do what the student expects! A role shift by the teacher often brings about a change of behavior in the student.

Long (1977), a middle-school principal, reports how she used a role-shift approach in working with two girls who had been sent to her office for smoking. She asked them to get their cigarettes and invited them to smoke and enjoy themselves while she presented some data on the relationship between smoking and lung cancer. She also explained why she herself chose not to smoke. She even offered the students the privilege of smoking in her office if they could obtain parental permission to do so. The unexpected role shift by Long was successful. The two girls decided not to smoke and caused no further problems. Such role shifts are most successful when the adult/student relationship is preserved and communication remains open.

During Step 2, teachers are asked to react to old disruptive behaviors as if they were first-time occurrences. In other words, teachers are asked to discard old lectures and routines with which the students are already familiar. This is also a good time to start catching students in good behavior. In order to do so successfully, teachers need to know how to do three things: *look, wait,* and *reinforce.* Usually teachers look only when disruptive attention-getting behavior is occurring. Seldom do they have the patience to wait until students do something desirable. When good behavior does occur, a teacher could say "I like it when you do your work" or "I appreciate your help." Good teachers systematically call their students' parents at the rate of one to three families per week to inform them about the good things their children have been doing. Another method is sending Happygrams to parents about their children's progress.

A word of warning needs to be said about reinforcement. As with all of the steps proposed in the lesson plan, things seem to work better if the techniques are not overused. Many good ideas can have the opposite effect if used improperly. Reinforcement is a case in point. Levine and Fasnacht (1974) cite attribution theory to explain these reverse effects of reinforcement procedures. When people are paid for doing an activity, they may come to believe that the activity is worth doing only for money and any intrinsic value the activity may have had may soon be forgotten.

Perhaps the technique of the counseling paradox is the biggest change of pace that can be used in Step 2. This technique capitalizes on the rebellious attitude of the student caught in a power struggle. To the student who is able to perform at higher levels but refuses to do so, the counselor might say "My long educational experience tells me that the prognosis in your case is pretty bad and that there isn't much hope of improvement." Often the rebellious student will work hard to prove the counselor wrong.

The counseling paradox seemingly flies in the face of the data generated by Rosenthal and Jacobson (1968) and others, which have demonstrated the significant effects expectations have on behavior. However, Frankl (1962), who originated the concept of paradoxical intention, and Watzlawick, Weakland, and Fish (1974), who have researched the technique more recently, emphasize that such an approach is one way of harnessing the student's rebellion toward achieving a positive change. A powerful source of energy such as rebellion need not be defeated and certainly not wasted. Of course, the counseling paradox may not be appropriate for defeated students who lack self-confidence but who are making sincere efforts to improve their performance. It should be noted that various paradoxical strategies have been designed to treat a variety of situations not involving the rebellious person (see Watzlawick et al., 1974). One elementary school teacher reports helping students rid themselves of hiccups by asking them to hiccup loud enough so that she can hear them and keep track of the frequency of the hiccups. Invariably the hiccups promptly stop.

Step 3

If Steps 1 and 2 have not succeeded in bringing about positive change, a third step is suggested. The teacher should make a list of the opportunities available in the classroom or school that would permit the student to have a better day tomorrow. Here are some of these opportunities:

1. Providing classroom jobs for the student to do
2. Playing ball with the student
3. Spending 20 seconds a day with the student
4. Giving the student choices in how to complete learning tasks (especially good for the power seeker)
5. Asking the student's opinion about something relevant to both teacher and student
6. Listening to the student talk about personal interests and concerns
7. Calling the student's parents when he or she has done something good or has had a good day

The Counseling Phase

Should the relationship phase fail to bring about the desired behavior change in the problem student, the teacher should continue to build on the relationship that was established during the first three steps of the plan. The counseling phase, also having three steps, is directed toward the student's accepting responsibility for his or her behavior and for the consequences of such behavior. Considerable effort is made to teach students how to commit themselves to making and following a workable plan to solve their problems.

Step 4

Quiet correction is recommended for Step 4. If the teacher has not asked the student to stop the undesired behavior, he or she may do so now during a private conference. Nonverbal communication is also recommended for Step 4. Grandpa Swander, a retired businessman turned teacher-counselor, keeps the following sign posted in his room in Harlingen, Texas, "Are you listening to Winners or Losers?"

The use of threats and "why" questions has been found to be harmful when working with discipline problems. Threats increase the power struggle, and "why" questions produce excuses for unhelpful behavior.

One-sentence counseling is useful at this stage of the plan. Asking students "What are you doing?" is a good way to make them recognize helpful and unhelpful behavior. The question "How is this helping you finish your assignment?" has also been effective. The "could it be" questions, referred to earlier, are other good examples of one-sentence counseling strategies. Another helpful question is "Are you aware of how your behavior affects my teaching?" All of these questions emphasize the students' responsibility for their behaviors.

In Step 4, teachers are encouraged to continue catching students in good behavior by acknowledging desirable actions. It is recommended, however, that teachers not thank students for behaving responsibly as if this were a special favor.

Step 5

Here the emphasis is on rules. Again, teachers are encouraged to refrain from using "why" questions, because they direct the counseling focus toward finding excuses for behavior rather than toward establishing that people are responsible for what they do. "Why" questions, which are most useful for developing depth when learning subject matters, are best limited to academic discussions. Students are so accustomed to answering "why" questions for misbehavior that they give these answers automatically—even when they are asked "what" questions. Remember, "why" questions are contract questions. After asking why and receiving the student's answer, the teacher has no place to go, because the contract has been fulfilled. The counseling procedure for Step 5 begins by posing the following questions:

1. What did you do?
2. What is our rule?
3. Was your behavior against our rule?
4. What were you supposed to do?
5. Will you prepare and give me your plan for following our rules?

The questions can then be used to form a written and signed contract between student and teacher. Many of our teachers have reproduced these questions on ditto sheets to be used in place of "write-offs" (the punishment that has the student write 500 times "I will never throw another eraser in this room").

If your students say very little or nothing in response to the "what" questions, their silence may indicate that they are beginning to face the situation and are ready to develop a plan for change. The emphasis here is on rules—but on *our* rules. The use of the above "what" questions is not necessarily an indication of effective counseling. However, the procedure should increase the teacher's effectiveness in working with behavior problems. Remember that the process may be repeated if the student's plan doesn't work. Refrain from asking for reasons or excuses and also from punishing students for not following their plans. Logical consequences for failure to follow one's plan will generally suffice.

Step 6

Glasser's (1965) reality-therapy approach is helpful for building responsibility and a sense of commitment to meet the contract's terms. The following questions are used:

1. What are you doing?
2. How does this help you? Others? Me?
3. If what you are doing is not helpful to anyone, what could you do, instead, that might be helpful?
4. When do you plan to start?

Develop these questions into written contracts, just as suggested in Step 5. Such contracts may be helpful at this point, because the procedure indicates that the student has the ability and power to make a good plan. Here, too, the teacher or counselor can help the student work out a personal plan to improve the situation. Once again, it is not helpful to lecture about the student's old faults. ask for excuses, or punish when the contract is broken. The most effective course of action is simply to tear up the old contract and ask the student to write a new one that has a better chance to be implemented. The contract's original, as well as its carbon copies, should be signed by all parties involved (Thompson & Poppen, 1972).

The Time-Out Phase

The time-out phase is designed for those students whose behavior has not improved enough during the first two phases. Steps 7 through 10, which make up the third phase, are designed to demonstrate more vividly the consequences of misbehavior. These steps are based on the same principle that lies behind the various techniques of isolation that our society adopts when irresponsible behavior occurs—techniques ranging from ignoring the action to rejection and, finally, incarceration of the person.

Step 7

Four levels of isolation have been researched for use in the school and classroom. In Step 7, two in-class time-out procedures are recommended. The first of these procedures is "seat 1 and seat 2." Seat 1 is the student's regular seat; seat 2 is located in the back of the room but not out of sight of the class group. If a student is busy doing something else (for example, working on a car model) when the class is supposed to be doing a mathematics assignment, the teacher quietly reminds the student that the model will have to be done in seat 2 because seat 1 is reserved for students working on their mathematics. However, the student will be allowed to return to seat 1—and, therefore, rejoin the group—when he or she makes a commitment to work on mathematics. This isolation technique, like all others in the time-out phase, is based on the premise that most students (especially the attention getters) prefer being with their group rather than alone for significant periods of time.

The second in-class time-out procedure is the "quiet corner." This isolation technique is designed for the student who "entertains" the small group of classmates in his or her immediate vicinity, and it is aimed at separating the "clown" from the audience. This is done by putting the student in a quiet corner, which is nothing more than one of the three or four study carrels in the classroom. The quiet-corner carrels (constructed from old refrigerator cartons or bookcases) are designed to put the student out of the audience's sight.

Teachers are encouraged to follow the use of seat 2 and the quiet corner with a plan, written by the student, for correcting the misbehavior. The student is given two choices: to be with the group and behave or to be outside and sit alone. Remember: seat 2 and the quiet corner are not punishment centers or dunce's seats. As a matter of fact, to be most effective, these places should also serve as enrichment spots, with a desk and a chair, as well as books, puzzles, and games. The goal is to keep the misbehaving student separated from the group—nothing more. All students and the teacher can choose to go to the quiet corner, but disrupters are obliged to go there. When a student misbehaves, the teacher sends him or her to the quiet corner firmly but with no discussion. Isolation procedures have the dual purpose of allowing teacher and class to do their work without interference and of teaching students that certain behaviors will isolate them from others (Thompson & Poppen, 1972).

Step 8

If the previous seven steps have failed, it may be time to move to one of the out-of-class time-out procedures such as sending the student to a time-out room, crisis-intervention classroom, half-way-house classroom, or the school office. Some students are classroom clowns and need to be completely separated from their audience. Here, too, each time-out occurrence is followed by the student's written plan for engaging in more helpful behavior in the classroom. If the school office is used as a time-out spot, it is important to shift the focus from punishment to planning. Remember that the utilization of the school office as a punishment technique is probably on the list of techniques that don't work, as are many other punishment strategies. Therefore, a change of pace is achieved by making the school office a comfortable resting place complete with magazines, books, and so on.

The time-out procedure begins with a designated cooling-off period, continues with development of a plan by the student, and concludes with a short conference between principal and student. The conference with the principal works best when the counseling formats outlined in Steps 5 and 6 are used in conjunction with written contracts. Essentially, the principal assists the student in writing a plan for getting back into and remaining in the classroom.

Step 9

When all school-based time-out procedures fail to teach the student the subject of discipline, a home- or community-based time-out procedure is recommended. It is difficult for some students to spend an entire day at school without infringing on someone else's rights. Then a contract is written with the student outlining the conditions under which he or she may remain at school. Breach of the contract terms results in the teacher's saying "You did well up to now, and maybe you'll do well for a little longer tomorrow. See you then." Depending on the circumstances, the teacher may ask the student's parents to pick up the child or simply ask the student to leave. Students receive as many benefits from the contract as teachers do. For example, no one lectures or paddles the student. Students merely return the next day and try to stay in school as long as they are able. The school may count these students present for the day, since they are participating in individualized programs of study.

All time-out procedures are based on logical consequences of behavior rather than on illogical punishment. Punishment is permissive, since it often removes the necessity for the student to face the natural consequences of his or her behavior. Glasser (1974) refers to the home-based time-out procedure as a tolerance day for students who are out of control. Thompson and Poppen (1972) refer to the process as systematic isolation. Parental involvement is highly desirable for this step, and often the parents' assistance is needed in developing the plan.

When it is not feasible to use the student's home as a time-out place, other locations may be considered. Neighborhood church staffs may agree to work with the school and take "time-out students" for the remainder of the school day. The students can often do volunteer work at the church or as teacher aides in day-school programs. Successful involvement with day-school children is one way for older students to gain self-esteem. The same is true of tutorial programs in which "problem students" help younger students in need of remedial assistance.

Other alternatives to home-based time-out include boys clubs and girls clubs. Frequently neighborhood volunteers agree to work with "time-out students" in their own homes when these students have to leave school for the day. The high school open-campus concept seems to be another good alternative for the out-of-school time-out procedure. The open campus allows students to remain on the school grounds even though they have been asked to leave class for the day. Perhaps the best alternative is the student study lounge, which is supervised by an adult for the purpose of allowing "time-out students" an opportunity to complete class assignments. Another time-out procedure utilizes the youth-services division of the local police department. The plainclothes youth-services staff will work with students if the school is unable to find a place on the school grounds or in the community where they can be when not in class.

Step 10

When the preceding nine steps fail, it is not enough for teachers, counselors, and principals to say that they did their best. There is still one last effort they can make to keep the students in a meaningful school program and to teach them discipline—a field trip to the juvenile court. Although the students may already have participated in court proceedings, the field trip could still include a conference with the judge and the development of additional plans for returning to school. Students may behave better just to avoid having to write new plans.

It may also be helpful to include a tour of the correctional facilities, complete with interviews with inmates, to help students decide whether they want to end up as inmates themselves. Educators have an obligation to try to make the students aware of the possible consequences of their behavior. Field trips to juvenile detention centers and prisons may serve this purpose well. Teenage delinquents in Woodbridge, New Jersey, are sent on field trips to Rahway State Prison to learn about incarceration from inmates serving life terms. As one convicted murderer serving a life term put it, "I'm 45 years old now, and I know I'm never going to see the streets again. Here we're all dying to get out, and you guys are pounding on the doors saying 'Let us in!' The Hollywood image of prison doesn't tell you about gang rapes and suicides. That happens all the time here, and you punks are fresh meat!" A visit to a prison can teach a great deal about behavioral consequences.

Finally, the school personnel may decide that certain students will best be served by finding alternative school programs better suited to their situations. Perhaps another school could break the learning of discipline down into even smaller steps with longer trial periods for each step. We wish to say, however, that thus far, out of the 132 students who have been on the program we just outlined, only one has been sent to another school. This particular student was making gains in the regular school program but was placed in a residential center because of family problems.

SUMMARY

This chapter has presented four counseling and guidance approaches for teaching discipline to students:

1. Using logical consequences with the four goals of misbehavior
2. Using classroom meetings for problem solving
3. Using a counseling-and-contract approach based on reality therapy
4. Using an individualized ten-step lesson plan for teaching discipline

The ten-step lesson plan, which combines most of the ideas presented in the other three approaches, is a complete system for teaching discipline to problem students who, for one reason or another, have not learned from other approaches.

Two common disciplinary procedures have been omitted from this chapter— paddling and the three-day suspension. Our research indicates that neither is truly effective.

To be more specific, paddling has proven effective with only one type of student—the good student. If the teacher paddles a good student once, he or she will never have to do it again. (And, we wish to add, probably there was no need to paddle this student in the first place.) Furthermore, vice-principals and principals who keep accurate records will tell you that there is more paddling in the spring than in the fall and that it is always the same students who get paddled over and over again. If paddling worked and students learned their lesson, the need for paddling should tail off by spring and principals would certainly not be paddling the same students time and time again. Finally, as we remarked earlier, how does paddling prepare the student for life outside of the school building? In our society we no longer use the whipping pillory and public floggings as consequences for irresponsible behavior. We use, instead, logical consequences and isolation, and that's what we should use in school.

As for the three-day school suspension, besides being generally ineffective, this procedure thrives on punishment rather than on logical consequences. For example, students are given automatic zero grades for each day they miss a subject—an almost impossible barrier to overcome if the students are trying to make a passing grade. The result is generally failure for the remainder of the year. And the best way to create discipline problems is to have a lot of failure in your school. Furthermore, the parents are punished along with their children. A common procedure is to ask the parents to accompany their child to school at the end of the three-day suspension. This often results in financial loss for the parent who is forced to miss work and a day's pay. Students are better off shouldering the logical consequences of their behavior! And, if they are able to make up their schoolwork on their own time, they should be given credit for it. However, they will have to do it under the handicap of missing the material covered in class. As noted earlier, we believe that systematic exclusion on a day-to-day basis is more effective and logical than the automatic three-day suspension.

Finally, to stress again a point we made before, it may be next to impossible to teach discipline in a bad classroom or in a bad school. If school is a place where nobody (students, faculty, and administration) wants to be and where nothing meaningful happens, how can one get the students to be respectful and responsible? Respect and responsibility must originate from the school program and from the faculty if we want our students to model and learn these qualities.

Chapter Nine

GROUP COUNSELING AND GUIDANCE MEETINGS FOR THE CLASSROOM

The developmental guidance activities we have presented in this book (and other similar ones) can be approached by teachers and counselors from a different angle. As we hope to show in the following discussion, this approach offers many advantages. We are referring to classroom counseling and guidance meetings—more specifically, to a sequence of seven types of meetings. We shall discuss this sequence by posing a series of questions.

What Are the Seven Types of Meetings?

1. Involvement meetings. The first type of meeting is aimed at building student involvement with school and with other students. Students learn that they belong to the group.

2. Rules and responsibilities meetings. These meetings deal with class rules and responsibilities. The teacher asks for suggestions and ideas about rules to be adopted, ways of working within the rules, changes to be made, and new rules that need to be established. The teacher also discusses classroom responsibilities and asks students what jobs they would like to

Ms. Judy Boser contributed to the writing of this chapter.

157

Group counseling lends itself to developing problem-solving strategies and decision making.

perform and what free-time activities they prefer. A contract between teacher and class may be drawn: "We, the students, would like to _____. I, the teacher, will _____." Rules meetings allow the teacher to share power as well as responsibilities with the class. Students learn that they can participate in the functioning of the classroom.

3. Thinking meetings. Thinking meetings are meant to increase the students' thinking and verbal abilities and to maintain involvement. The specific purpose of the meeting is to share ideas and thoughts. Students learn that their ideas are worthy of the teacher's and the class' attention. They also learn that expressing ideas stimulates thinking, which in turn stimulates curiosity and learning. Another advantage of these meetings is that they can help the teacher determine the level of student learning for the purpose of planning and evaluating instruction.

4. Values-clarification meetings. The goal of these meetings is to have students see more clearly their personal values and develop tolerance for the values of others in the class. These meetings also help students realize that their values are instrumental to the goals they set for themselves and to the decisions they make.

5. Hypothetical dilemmas. This type of meeting relates to the development of plans of action for various hypothetical problem situations or value conflicts that the students may encounter. One intention of these meetings is to promote divergent thinking instead of a single, right solution. Another intention is to give students experience in dealing with hypothetical situations that can serve as a foundation for effective action when facing real problems.

6. *Actual problem solving.* In the sixth type of meeting the class deals with real problems that develop in the classroom or with a decision they need to make as a group. A variation of this meeting is to use the group to give an individual member support and assistance in solving a problem or in changing a behavior.

7. *Class council.* The class council is the procedure through which the group "governs" itself. It is essentially a more formal variation of the problem-solving meeting and of the rules meeting. These two types of meetings are replaced with the class council whenever the teacher thinks that the class is ready for formal elections and self-government.

What Are the Sequence and Duration of the Meetings?

The following chart illustrates the sequence of the meetings and suggests how long each type of meeting should last. The time is not prescriptive; the teacher or counselor should move on to the next type of meeting only after the objectives of the previous ones have been reached.

September	Type 1 (involvement) and type 2 (rules)
October	Type 3 (thinking)
November	Type 4 (values clarification)
December	Type 5 (hypothetical dilemmas)
January	Type 6 (actual problem solving)
February	Type 7 (class council)

Should the Teacher Have Conducted All Seven Types of Meetings by Midyear?

Not necessarily. Some groups never develop sufficiently during the school year to be able to handle meetings 6 and 7. Teachers and counselors are cautioned not to try type-6 meetings until the students have been successful with the other types of meetings. The students need the skills they learn in these other meetings to work effectively with types 6 and 7. Even if a class never moves to meetings 6 and 7, the students may still be able to gain considerable benefit from the other types of meetings. Also, some groups can productively spend more time with meetings 1, 2, and 3 than is indicated in the diagram above. Teachers should establish the class council as a continuation of rules meetings; meetings on actual problem solving should be held only when teachers think the class is ready. Type-3, -4, and -5 meetings should be used periodically throughout the school year to maintain student involvement, to help students reconsider personal values, and to provide additional training in problem-solving skills.

Why Should the Sequence Be Followed, and What Is the Rationale for the Seven Types of Meetings?

Considerable research has been conducted about the stages of development of an effective group and about the positive influences of an effective group on the learning of the group members. Schmuck and Schmuck (1975) draw a parallel between the development of the group by stages and the systematic development of a child into an adult. (It should be kept in mind that any group can be blocked at a particular stage of development.) The chart below shows how the seven meetings correlate to these stages.

The seven types of meetings	Four stages of group development (goals to be attained)			
	Stage 1: Inclusion and membership	Stage 2: Establishing shared influence and collaborative decision making	Stage 3: Pursuing individual and academic goals	Stage 4: Self-renewal; adapting to change
Involvement	S			
Class rules and responsibilities		S		
Thinking	D			
Values clarification	M		S	
Hypothetical dilemmas			S	
Actual problem solving		D	D	
Class council		M	M	D/M

S = Started   D = Developed   M = Maintained

The empty- (or open-) chair technique is useful in group counseling for decision making and rehearsal of new behaviors.

In the chart, the goal of each type of meeting in relation to the four stages of group development is indicated by S (the attainment of the goal is started with this type of meeting), D (the attainment of the goal is developed with this type of meeting), or M (the attainment of the goal is maintained with this type of meeting).

What Are Some Examples of the Guidance Activities Used in Each Type of Meeting?

The following is a list of activities, already discussed in the preceding chapters, that can help teacher and counselor plan a sequence of class meetings and guidance activities for the school year.

Suggested Activities for Building Involvement

Suggested Activity for Class Council

How Much Time Is Required for Effective Classroom Meetings and Guidance Activities?

Initially teacher and counselor will need a few hours for planning and organizing the sequence of activities to be used during the school year. Once the overall planning is done, the time needed to organize the individual activities should be no greater than that required for any other class activity, such as a reading or history lesson. Some additional time may be needed for self-evaluation or feedback from an observer, perhaps the school counselor or another teacher.

Because most of the activities require 15 to 30 minutes and because it is suggested that teachers hold one to three meetings each week, approximately one-half to one and a half hours a week will be spent actually carrying out the meetings. It is recommended that younger students not participate in long meetings and that students in departmentalized instructional settings not attend meetings for more than one and a half hours per week.

How Can a Teacher Be Sure that the Meetings Are Being Conducted Appropriately?

First, the teacher should check the Group-Leadership Checklist presented in Chapter Two. Second, he or she should ask the students to give evaluations of the meetings, using some form of questionnaire of the kind illustrated on p. 96. The Semantic Differential in Appendix C could also be used. With young students, a simple show of hands will do. No matter what kind of evaluation is used, some evaluation is necessary, because teachers need to know whether the meetings achieve the desired results. Also, since students generally give the meetings high ratings, the evaluation offers teachers much-needed reinforcement for their efforts.

What Other Evaluation May Be Useful?

The Sentence-Completion Form in Appendix C may be used as a pre- and posttest. The Semantic Differential may also be used early in the school year and then again toward the middle and end of the year. The Sociometric Test (Instruments 3 and 4 in Appendix C) is an especially useful measure of involvement. It can be used frequently to determine whether each student in the class is indeed a part of the class.

What Other Additional Resources Can Be Used in Planning a Complete Curriculum of Guidance Activities?

The following books and articles are categorized according to the area in which they will be of greatest assistance, since most of them contain material that is helpful for planning activities in a variety of areas. The list is by no means exhaustive. The main criteria for inclusion were practicality and economy.

Involvement Meetings

Howe, L., & Howe, M. *Personalizing Education.* New York: Hart, 1975.

Lindberg, R., Bartell, S., & Estes, G. "Measured Outcomes of Involvement in the Classroom." *The School Counselor,* 1977, *24*(3), 148-155.

Stanford, G. *Developing Effective Classroom Groups: A Practical Guide for Teachers.* New York: Hart, 1977.

Rules Meetings

Gordon, T. *Teacher Effectiveness Training* (especially Chapter 9). New York: McKay, 1974.

Thinking Meetings

Chase, L. *The Other Side of the Report Card: A How-to-Do-It Program for Affective Education* (especially Chapter 4). Pacific Palisades, Calif.: Goodyear, 1975.

Values-Clarification Meetings

Canfield, J., & Wells, H. *100 Ways to Enhance Self-Concept in the Classroom.* Englewood Cliffs, N.J.: Prentice-Hall, 1976.

Simon, S. *Values Clarification: A Handbook of Practical Strategies for Teachers and Students.* New York: Hart, 1972.

Simon, S., & Olds, S. *Helping Your Child Learn Right from Wrong.* New York: Simon & Schuster, 1976.

Hypothetical Dilemmas

Furness, P. *Role-Play in the Elementary School.* New York: Hart, 1976.

Galbraith, R., & Jones, T. *Moral Reasoning: Teaching Strategies for Adapting Kohlberg to the Classroom.* Anoka, Minn.: Greenhaven Press, 1976.

Hawley, R. *Value Exploration through Role-Playing: Practical Strategies for Use in the Classroom.* New York: Hart, 1975.

Actual Problem Solving

Schmuck, R., & Schmuck, P. *Group Process in the Classroom.* Dubuque, Iowa: Brown, 1975.

Class Council

Dreikurs, R., Grunwald, B., & Pepper, F. *Maintaining Sanity in the Classroom: Illustrated Teaching Techniques.* New York: Harper & Row, 1971.

Chapter Ten

IN-SERVICE
EDUCATION WORKSHOP
IN REALITY THERAPY

Elementary and secondary school counselors are frequently asked to assist the administration in providing effective continuing-education or professional-growth activities for teachers and other staff members. On other occasions, even though counselor assistance is not requested, the counselor may want to take the initiative in offering relevant in-service education.

This chapter presents the format for a short-term program for teaching the reality-therapy process to teachers and other school personnel. Since students naturally share concerns and problems with their favorite teachers, it is important that teachers have at least some minimal counseling skills in addition to whatever good interpersonal-communication skills they already possess. It is up to the teachers, of course, to decide if and when they want to refer a student to the counselor for special help. Aside from other considerations, teachers seldom have sufficient time or even an appropriate place to do extensive counseling.

The learning and use of counseling skills can make teachers more effective in their day-to-day functions and can also help them build a set of correct expectations about school counseling. When, because of their own experience, teachers know what counseling is all about, they also know that referred students will be helped rather than manipulated or punished.

Session 1

The first meeting is designed to present an overview of reality therapy and counseling and to help the workshop participants learn the basic assumptions of the system (see Chapters Two and Eight). A description of the procedure for presenting such an overview follows. The later meetings are devoted to the individual steps that constitute the process of reality counseling.

Counselors may be responsible for conducting some in-service education with the faculty.

Activity: Overview of Reality Therapy

Purpose: To learn the reality-therapy process.

Group size: Any even number.

Time required: 60 to 90 minutes.

Materials: Ten sheets of paper and two pencils per dyad.

Physical setting: Movable chairs to allow the group to work in dyads.

Procedure: The procedure for presenting the overview is the following:

1. Teach the eight steps in the reality-therapy process and the four basic questions utilized in reality counseling.

   The eight steps (reality therapy):
   a. Involvement (building the relationship)
   b. Focus on present behavior
   c. Making value judgments
   d. Developing a plan
   e. Commitment
   f. No excuses
   g. No punishment
   h. Never give up

   The four questions (reality counseling):
   a. What are you doing?
   b. How is your behavior helping you?
   c. What could you do, instead, that would help you?
   d. What will you do, and when will you start?

2. Demonstrate the reality-counseling process with a volunteer (could be a real or a role-played situation).
3. Ask the members to select a partner—preferably someone they don't know well. (Pairing of new acquaintances seems to work better in all dyad activities.)
4. One partner assumes the counselor's role and the other the client's role.
5. Each dyad writes a script for a reality-counseling interview by using the paper/pencil role-play process. Communication takes place only in writing. The client begins by writing a response and passing the paper to the counselor. The counselor writes down his or her response and returns the paper to the client, who in turn writes a reply and gives the paper back to the counselor. The back-and-forth writing process continues until the leader interrupts it or the two participants think they are finished.
6. The scripts are read by both partners at the end of the session for group- and self-evaluation.
7. Reverse roles and repeat. The scripts provide an accurate account of how well the participants have grasped the basic concepts of the reality-counseling process.

Resources:

The Identity Society, by W. Glasser (New York: Harper & Row, 1972).

Reality Therapy, by W. Glasser (New York: Harper & Row, 1965).
Schools without Failure, by W. Glasser (New York: Harper & Row, 1969).

Session 2

The second meeting concentrates on investigating involvement as a concept and practicing ways of building involvement in the school and in teacher/student relationships. Activities presented in this book that are appropriate for practicing involvement are: the Group-Strengths Test, the Compliment Game, the Strengths-Trade Game, Strengths Listing, and Strengths Badge (all in Chapter Three) and Becoming a Reinforcing Person (in Chapter Four).

One activity, not presented elsewhere in this book and based on a concept borrowed from transactional analysis, is very helpful in determining changes one might want to make in a relationship or setting. This activity, Four Types of Strokes, builds positive involvement. A description follows.

Activity: The Four Types of Strokes

Purpose: To learn the four basic types of strokes, or interactions, that can occur between people; to determine which types of strokes are preferred by the workshop participants; to examine the types of strokes the participants most frequently use in their classrooms and various school situations.

Group size: Any number.

Time required: 30 to 45 minutes.

Materials: Blackboard or transparencies of points a-g and strokes graph; paper and pencil for each participant.

Physical setting: Lecture room with enough flexibility to allow group members to form dyads.

Procedure: Here is the sequence of steps the activity requires:

1. Explain the following points. (Answers to points *d, e, f,* and *g* appear in parentheses.) A transparent overlay facilitates the discussion.

a. What are strokes?
   Any recognition, such as
   a touch
   a look
   a word

   _____

   _____ (ask participants to list others)
b. What types of strokes are there?
   positive (+)
   negative (–)
c. Some strokes are conditional and tell us about our competencies.
d. There are conditional positive strokes.
   There are conditional _____ strokes. (negative)
e. "I certainly enjoy dancing with you; you're sure fun to dance with"
   is a _____ _____ stroke. (conditional positive)
f. "I hate it when you drink too much"
   is a _____ _____ stroke. (conditional negative)
g. Some strokes are unconditional.
   "I love you" is an _____ _____ stroke. (unconditional positive)
   "You are stupid" is an _____ _____ stroke. (unconditional negative)

2. Have people form dyads and practice giving each other the various types of strokes. Discuss whether the strokes make them feel comfortable or uncomfortable. Which stroke do they like best? Ask the participants to write examples of the four types of strokes and share some of them with the group.
3. Ask the group members to answer the question "Who strokes you?" by listing the people who do so. (Ask them whether they included themselves.)
4. Have the participants complete two or three strokes graphs (see Figure 10-1).

   a. What types of strokes do you *give*?
   b. What types of strokes do you *get*?
   c. What types of strokes are usually given where you work? at home?
   d. The participants may be asked whether they are satisfied with their strokes graphs and, if they are not, what they can do to change the situation.

Session 3

The third meeting is devoted to identifying behaviors and making value judgments. More specifically, the workshop teaches participants to concentrate on asking and responding to the questions "What are you doing?" and "Is it helpful?" Three activities are suggested for this meeting, but it is recommended that only two be used. What Are You Doing in Your Life? or Extending and Enriching Your Life may be used, followed by Time Structuring. This last activity requires a homework period between sessions 3 and 4 and a follow-up discussion during session 4.

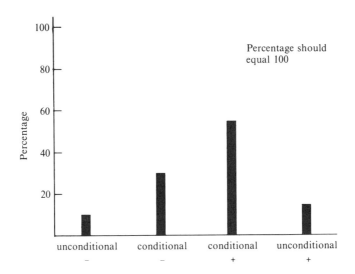

Figure 10-1. Strokes graph.

Activity: What Are You Doing in Your Life?

Purpose: To list and examine present behaviors.

Group size: 6 to 8 members per subgroup or demonstration group.

Time required: 30 minutes.

Materials: Paper and pencil for each participant.

Physical setting: Room with flexible seating.

Procedure: Go through the following steps:

1. Ask the group members to write down a list of five things they are doing now in their lives.
2. A small group (6 to 8) of participants share their lists while you demonstrate how to focus on present behaviors rather than on the reasons for the behaviors.
3. The participants watch your demonstration and note their observations or questions. After the demonstration, comments and questions are rated as either focusing or not focusing on behaviors. (*Note:* You may want to include some inappropriate—that is, not focusing—questions to see whether the participants observe properly. If you do include inappropriate questions, write them down or use some procedure to remember them. This will allow a comparison between the inappropriate responses actually given and the responses indicating that the participants noticed them. An audio- or videotape may be useful for validating audience observations.)
4. The participants are asked to rank their five behaviors on a 5-to-1 scale from most helpful to least helpful. After having ranked the behaviors, the members write a statement about how the behaviors are helpful to them and to others. Some of the rankings and rationales are then shared with the group.

Activity: Extending and Enriching Your Life

Purpose: To examine and become aware of present behavior patterns; to learn a self-counseling strategy for finding new ways of extending and enriching one's own life.

Group size: Any number.

Time required: 30 minutes.

Materials: Paper and pencils.

Physical setting: Space for individual work and for group discussion, with 6 to 10 members in each group.

Procedure: The activity consists of three steps:

1. Ask the participants to divide a sheet of paper into two columns and list in one column all the things they are doing to extend their lives and in the second column all the things they are doing to enrich their lives. Some items will, of course, be included in both columns.
2. After the participants have completed their lists, have them form small

discussion groups for the purpose of presenting their findings to the whole group. The participants should also make value judgments about the appropriateness and usefulness of the things they are doing.
3. The information shared in the discussions can be utilized by the participants to commit themselves in the form of a contract to changing some of their behaviors—for example, quitting smoking.

Activity: Time Structuring

Purpose: To build awareness of how one spends one's time.

Group size: Any number.

Time required: 30 to 60 minutes for discussion of homework assignment. Such assignment is done over a seven-day period.

Materials: Paper, pencils, and diary-type notebooks.

Physical setting: Groups of 6 to 30 can work on the discussion following the homework assignment.

Procedure: Here are the directions for this activity:

1. Ask the group members to keep a journal-type record of how they spend each hour of the week between group meetings.
2. After a week of record keeping, the participants are asked to construct a pie graph depicting how they spend each day. Figure 10-2 is an example of such a graph.

8   hours work
8   hours sleep
2   hours watching TV
2   hours reading
2   hours playing tennis
1½ hours eating
½ hour showering and
    getting dressed

Figure 10-2. Pie graph.

3. The pie graphs are displayed in the group room for the purpose of comparing similarities and differences in the behaviors of the participants.
4. A group discussion follows, focusing on the participants' feelings about their behavior patterns.
5. A modification of the above procedure is to provide the group members with wrist counters so they can obtain specific counts of undesirable behaviors such as smoking or snacking.

Session 4

The purpose of the fourth meeting is to teach specific skills in planning and commitment. After the participants have become aware of behaviors they find unsatisfactory, they are encouraged to formulate a plan to change the undesirable behaviors. The formulation of a plan requires a thorough search for alternatives. Leader and participants must engage in *divergent* thinking (brainstorming) to identify as many alternatives as possible. Evaluation of alternatives, or convergent thinking, is withheld until the complete list of alternatives is compiled. Once the most appropriate plan has been identified, the plan is put in writing so the participant can make a commitment to it.

Two techniques—the Brainstorming Wheel and Plan Writing—are suggested for this session. The primary objective of these activities is to permit the participants to become familiar enough with the activities to be able to carry them out with their student(s) as a part of the reality-therapy process.

Activity: Brainstorming Wheel

Purpose: To make the divergent-thinking process as productive as possible in researching and finding alternatives.

Procedure: The activity consists of the following two parts:

1. Take a blank sheet of paper and write the problem or concern in the middle of the page. Draw four to six circles around the page near the outer margins. The objective is to fill the circles with alternatives. Both you and the participants may write in alternatives. However, you should not write less than two alternatives, thereby allowing the participants to

assume the responsibility for choosing between the two ideas. In some cases the participants may be left alone in order to have "time-out" to think of alternatives. In other cases they may be given the chance to consult with someone they think may have some useful ideas.

Leader's Checklist (with appropriate answers)

Yes   No

____   ____   Problem or concern written on paper. (yes)

____   ____   Circles drawn on page. (yes)

____   ____   Leader suggested two ideas. (yes, if needed)

____   ____   Leader nonjudgmental of participants' ideas. (yes)

____   ____   Leader sold own ideas. (no)

____   ____   Leader encouraged guessing or vague ideas. (yes)

____   ____   Ideas were evaluated before wheel was completed. (no)

2. The second part of the activity permits you to ascertain that the participants know how to get from where they are to where they want to be. In order to make the route to the desired goal more specific and concrete, a sequencing technique is suggested. Take a blank sheet of paper and write the goal in the upper right-hand corner. Then put the number 1 in the lower left-hand corner and write "Where you are now" next to it. Write the numbers 2, 3, 4, and 5 diagonally across the page (see Figure 10-3). Suggest that there are logical steps the participants need to take in order to reach the goal.

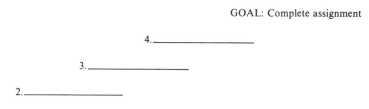

GOAL: Complete assignment

4._____

3._____

2._____

1. Where you are now.

Figure 10-3. Goal: Complete a project assignment by next Monday.

Some of the logical steps that need to be taken are likely to be (a) understand assignment, (b) determine specific time to work on the project, and (c) obtain the necessary materials for writing the final report. It is possible that the sequencing of these steps will result in the identification of additional tasks to be completed; therefore, more than five steps may be listed on the sheet. The sequencing technique assures the leader that the participant has definite direction and knows what steps should be taken to reach the goal. It is important to remember that the sequencing should be developed cooperatively.

As a part of the workshop experience, each participant may be asked to role-play the process of making a plan, using the sequencing technique with another participant who presents a hypothetical goal.

Activity: Plan Writing

Purpose: To facilitate the development of a plan leading to behavioral change.

Group size: Any number of people working in dyads.

Time required: 40 to 50 minutes.

Materials: Writing paper and carbon paper for each dyad, pencils or pens, and a list of the characteristics of a good plan (see below) for each participant.

Physical setting: People working in dyads.

Procedure: Here is the sequence of steps required by this activity:

1. Explain the characteristics of good and bad plans and give examples of each.
2. Present and discuss the Characteristics of a Good Plan (see below).
3. Break groups into dyads. Ask the participants to think of a goal they would like to set for themselves.
4. With one partner taking the role of the leader and the other the role of participant, work out a plan that meets the suggested characteristics of a good plan. Switch roles after the first plan is developed.
5. Original and carbon copies of each contract are signed by both parties, with each party keeping a copy.
6. Each dyad partner checks the progress of the other on specified dates.

Characteristics of a Good Plan

1. Choose a behavior you wish to change—one that is both observable and measurable.
2. Take note of the setting and situation in which you are most likely to perform the behavior. Avoiding or changing the setting may be helpful.
3. Use the Brainstorming Wheel to select a procedure for reaching the desired goal.

4. Maintain an accurate account of your behavior in order to evaluate the effectiveness of your procedure or technique in attaining your goal.
5. Once your goal has been achieved, you may wish to arrange a plan for maintaining the goal—for example, a weekly check on the status of your performance level.
6. Set up a procedure for rewarding yourself when you follow your contract plan, make honest progress, and meet your objectives.
7. Written contracts have proven to be more effective than verbal contracts, especially if other people are involved in your contract.
8. Develop positive rather than negative statements of the goals you hope to attain.
9. Renegotiate contracts that are not working.

Session 5

The final meeting is designed to help the participants accept the fact that plans will not always be followed and that contracts will be broken. The leader doesn't give up but responds without either blaming or excusing the participant who made the plan. The focus should be on recycling the plan or looking for a plan that will work better. The leader's approach remains positive all the time. After completing the activity No Excuses, No Blame, No Punishment, it may be useful for the group to return to the Overview activity done during the first meeting as a way of reviewing what they have learned about the reality-therapy process. Teachers and counselors need to define for themselves what "never give up" means. Generally, most professionals define "never give up" to mean that they will stick with the student longer than the student expects.

Activity: No Excuses, No Blame, No Punishment

Purpose: To help teachers learn the reality-counseling approach of no blaming, excusing, or punishing.

Group size: Triads.

Time required: 30 minutes.

Materials: A list of role-playing situations and one rating form per participant (see below).

Physical setting: Flexible seating arrangement to allow triad conversations.

Procedure: The directions for this activity are as follows:

1. Form triads.
2. Demonstrate the triad interaction: person A role-plays the student, person B role-plays the teacher or counselor, and person C observes and rates. Each person plays each part in order, as time allows.
3. The role playing is brief (3 to 5 minutes). Approximately 5 minutes are used for observer feedback about the rating form.
4. Audiotaped or videotaped replay and observation may be used if available; if so, time requirements should be doubled.

Examples of Role-Playing Situations

Tom has agreed to talk to Wallace about the possibility of getting some tutorial help in learning verb forms. The teacher who made the agreement with Tom knows that Tom never got in touch with Wallace. Role-play what the teacher could say or do, without excusing or blaming the student. (*Note:* The preferred approach would be for the teacher to ask "What happened when you talked to Wallace? Are you still interested in tutoring help? Are you still interested in talking to him? When will you do it?")

A student has agreed to complete a strengths list before coming to class today. The student comes to class without the list and claims that she forgot to bring it. Role-play what the teacher would say or do.

Observer's Rating Form for No Blame or Excuses

Write the essence of the teacher's response.	Rate each response as: *a* - appropriate and leading to new agreement *b* - blaming *c* - excuse accepted *d* - punitive, critical, or a put-down

REFERENCES

American Personnel and Guidance Association. *Personnel and Guidance Journal,* 1973, *51*(9).

American Psychological Association. *Periodically,* 1972, *3*(2).

Bechtol, W. *Individualizing instruction and keeping your sanity.* Chicago: Follett, 1973.

Branan, K. Ideas for opening up. *Scholastic Teacher,* 1972, *99,* 6-10.

Carkhuff, R. *Helping and human relations* (2 vols.). New York: Holt, Rinehart & Winston, 1969.

Carkhuff, R. *Human achievement, educational achievement, career achievement: Essential ingredients of elementary school guidance.* Paper presented at the Second Annual National Elementary School Guidance Conference, Louisville, Kentucky, March 30, 1973.

Coopersmith, S. *The antecedents of self-esteem.* San Francisco: W. H. Freeman, 1967.

Davis, G. *Psychology of problem solving.* New York: Basic Books, 1973.

Dinkmeyer, D., & Caldwell, E. *Developmental counseling and guidance: A comprehensive school approach.* New York: McGraw-Hill, 1970.

Dreikurs, R. *Psychology in the classroom* (2nd ed.). New York: Harper & Row, 1968.

Ellis, A. Teaching emotional education in the classroom. *School Health Review,* November 1969, 10-13.

Farrald, R., & Schamber, R. *A diagnostic and prescriptive technique: Handbook 1.* Sioux Falls, S.D.: Adapt Press, 1973.

Frankl, V. E. *Man's search for meaning: An introduction to logotherapy.* Boston: Beacon, 1962.

Ginott, H. *Between teacher and child.* New York: Macmillan, 1972.

Glasser, W. *Reality therapy.* New York: Harper & Row, 1965.

Glasser, W. *Schools without failure.* New York: Harper & Row, 1969.

Glasser, W. *The identity society.* New York: Harper & Row, 1972.

Glasser, W. A new look at discipline. *Learning,* 1974, *3,* 6-11.

Gum, M., Tamminen, A., & Smaby, M. Developmental guidance experiences. *Personnel and Guidance Journal,* 1973, *51,* 647-652.

Levine, F. M., & Fasnacht, G. Token rewards may lead to token learning. *American Psychologist,* 1974, *29,* 816-820.

Long, E. Smoke! smoke! smoke! smoke! *Creative Discipline,* 1977, *1,* 1-2.

Maslow, A. *Motivation and personality* (2nd ed.). New York: Harper & Row, 1970.

McClelland, D. C., & Steele, R. S. *Motivation workshops.* New York: General Learning Press, 1972.

Millman, J. Reporting student progress: A case for a criterion-reference marking system. *Phi Delta Kappan,* December 1970, 226-230.

Myrick, R. The counselor's workshop: Learning centers—An approach to developmental guidance. *Elementary School Guidance and Counseling,* October 1973, 58-63.

Nylen, D., Mitchell, J., & Stout, A. An experiment in cooperation. *Today's Education,* 1969, *58*(7), 57.

Peters, H., & Farwell, G. *Guidance: A developmental approach.* Chicago: Rand McNally, 1959.

Poppen, W. A., & Thompson, C. L. *School counseling: Theories and concepts.* Lincoln, Neb.: Professional Educators Publications, 1974.

Raths, L., Harmin, M., & Simon, S. *Values and teaching.* Columbus, Ohio: Merrill, 1966.

Robinson, R. *Why they love to learn.* Charlotte, N.C.: Heritage Printers, 1960.

Rogers, C. *Client-centered therapy.* Boston: Houghton Mifflin, 1951.

Rosenthal, R., & Jacobson, L. *Pygmalion in the classroom: Teacher expectation and pupils' intellectual development.* New York: Holt, Rinehart & Winston, 1968.

Sax, S., & Hollander, S. *Reality games.* New York: Popular Library, 1972.

Schmuck, R. A., & Schmuck, P. A. *Group processes in the classroom* (2nd ed.). Dubuque, Iowa: Brown, 1975.

Shallcross, D. Creativity: Everybody's business. *Personnel and Guidance Journal,* 1973, *51,* 623-626.

Simon, S., Howe, L., & Kirschenbaum, H. *Values clarification.* New York: Hart, 1972.

Thompson, C. L., & Cates, J. T. Why tutor? *Tennessee Education,* 1973, *3,* 5-10.

Thompson, C. L., & Cates, J. T. Teaching discipline to students: An individualized teaching-counseling approach. *Focus on Guidance,* 1976, *9,* 1-12.

Thompson, C. L., & Poppen, W. A. *For those who care: Ways of relating to youth.* Columbus, Ohio: Merrill, 1972.

Thompson, C. L., Prater, A. R., & Poppen, W. A. One more time: How do you motivate students? *Elementary School Guidance and Counseling,* 1974, *9,* 30-34.

Watzlawick, P., Weakland, C. E., & Fish, R. *Change: Principles of problem formation and problem resolution.* New York: Norton, 1974.

Appendix A

PROJECT-SCHOOL POPULATIONS AND DESCRIPTIONS

County	Population (1970 Census)	Percent of State Population	School Setting
Dickson	24,839	.053	Rural-agrarian
Lawrence	34,049	.079	Urban-agrarian
Macon	18,197	.04	Urban-industrial
Milan (city)	16,000	.03	Urban-industrial
Robertson	33,335	.077	Rural-agrarian
Unicoi	21,082	.041	Urban-industrial
Williamson	31,267	.07	Rural-industrial

County (Center)	School Population	Grades	Type of Building	Classroom Setting
Dickson (White Bluff)	5795 (513)	1-6	New	Self-contained
Lawrence (Ingram Sowell)	6828 (329)	1-6	Old	Self-contained
Macon (Central)	2550 (473)	5-8	New	Self-contained
Milan City (K.D. McKellar)	2372 (650)	4-6	Old	Self-contained
Robertson (Greenbrier)	7577 (651)	K-6	New	Open-spaced
Unicoi (Evans)	3632 (675)	1-6	New	Open-spaced
Williamson (Lipscomb)	7395 (946)	1-6	Old and new	Open-spaced, self-contained

EQUIPMENT NEEDS FOR THE GUIDANCE OFFICE

1	filmstrip projector
1	filmstrip-projector cart
1	mirror
1	record player
1	rug
1	typing table
1	typewriter
1	bulletin board and chalkboard combination
1	book truck
1	listening-station equipment
1	rocking chair
2	comfortable chairs for individual counseling or consultation
1	tape recorder
1	desk and chair
1	filing cabinet (5 drawers)
15	chairs for group counseling
1	parent-education kit or file
1	career-development kit or file
1	career-information file
1	college-information file
1	vocational-training information file

INSTRUMENTS FOR TESTING AND EVALUATION

INSTRUMENT 1
SENTENCE-COMPLETION FORM

Complete the following form about yourself. Be honest in your answers. *There are no right or wrong answers.*

1. When I look in the mirror ——————————————.
2. Many times I think I am ——————————————.
3. When I look at other boys and girls and then look at myself, I feel ——— ——————————————.
4. I often wish ——————————————.
5. If I could be someone else, I ——————————————.
6. My teacher thinks I am ——————————————.
7. I am best when ——————————————.
8. I am happiest when ——————————————.
9. What I like to do most is ——————————————.
10. Most of all I want to ——————————————.

   Note: Statements can be evaluated as positive (+1), neutral (0), or negative (-1). The student may score between -10 and +10.

INSTRUMENT 2
SEMANTIC DIFFERENTIAL

Put a check in the blank that tells how you feel about DOGS. For example, if you feel good about dogs, you put a check in the first blank:

GOOD   ✓__ __ __ __ __ __   BAD

If you feel pretty good about dogs, you put a check in the third blank:

GOOD   __ __ ✓__ __ __ __   BAD

If you don't like dogs, you put a check in the last blank:

GOOD   __ __ __ __ __ __ ✓__   BAD

Put a check in the blank that tells how you feel about SCHOOL.

GOOD	__	__	__	__	__	__	__	BAD
COLD	__	__	__	__	__	__	__	WARM
INTERESTING	__	__	__	__	__	__	__	BORING
WEAK	__	__	__	__	__	__	__	STRONG
HAPPY	__	__	__	__	__	__	__	SAD
UNFRIENDLY	__	__	__	__	__	__	__	FRIENDLY
IMPORTANT	__	__	__	__	__	__	__	UNIMPORTANT
WORTHLESS	__	__	__	__	__	__	__	VALUABLE
OPEN	__	__	__	__	__	__	__	CLOSED

Note: Scales are evaluated on a 1- to 7-point basis, with 7 being the highest score. The total score can be obtained by adding the scores for each scale. The range can be a score from 9 to 63. A low score indicates a negative attitude toward the place, activity, person, or thing in question. A high score indicates a positive attitude. The semantic differential is designed to measure one's attitude toward anything. The semantic differential presented above is designed to measure the child's attitude toward school. The same scale may be used to measure the child's attitude toward self, teachers, parents, or any other person, place, activity, or thing.

INSTRUMENT 3
SOCIOMETRIC TEST (A)

Date _____

Your number _____

Homeroom teacher _____

How I Feel about Others in My Class

We all have different feelings about other people. We like some people a lot, some a little bit, and some not at all. Sometimes we think that it is not proper or polite to dislike others, but, when we are really honest about it, we know that everyone has some negative feelings about somebody. There are some people you like a lot, and there are others you don't like at all. If the teacher knows the way you really feel about other students in your class, he or she can often plan things better. *There are no right or wrong answers.*

1. Which three students in this homeroom do you like the most? Using your class list with names and numbers, write the three numbers in the blanks.

Student's number

The three students I like most are: _____

_____

_____

2. Which three students do you like least? Write the numbers in the blanks.

The three students I like least are: _____

_____

_____

3. Which three students would you like to play with? Write the numbers in the blanks.

The three students I would like to play with are: _____

_____

_____

4. Which three students would you like to study with or work with on a school project? Write the numbers in the blanks.

The three students I would like to work with are: _____

_____

_____

INSTRUMENT 4
SOCIOMETRIC TEST (B)

1. List the three students in this classroom next to whom you would like to sit.

_____

_____

_____

2. List the three students you would like to have on a sports team with you.

_____

_____

_____

3. List the three students you would like to study with in a group.

_____

_____

_____

INSTRUMENT 5
PERSONAL-PROBLEM GOAL

My goal is _____

_____

First week	*Counselor's comments*
I achieved my goal _____	
I'm moving toward my goal (things are getting better)	
No progress _____	
I've changed my goal _____	
No longer a problem _____	
Second Week	
I achieved my goal _____	
I'm moving toward my goal _____ (things are getting better)	
No progress _____	
I've changed my goal _____	
No longer a problem _____	

INSTRUMENT 6
STUDENT-OBSERVATION FORM

Teacher _____

Three strengths of _____
    A.   _____
    B.   _____
    C.   _____

Inappropriate behavior (list two):
    A.   _____
    B.   _____

Frequency of inappropriate behavior:

M	T	W	T	F	M	T	W	T	F	M	T	W	T	F	M	T	W	T	F

INSTRUMENT 7
TEACHER'S RECORD OF STUDENT BEHAVIOR

Name of student ——————————————————————————
Date of observation ——————————————————————————
Reason for referral ——————————————————————————

	Monday	Tuesday	Wednesday	Thursday	Friday	Monday	Tuesday	Wednesday	Thursday	Friday	Monday	Tuesday	Wednesday	Thursday	Friday	Monday	Tuesday	Wednesday	Thursday	Friday	Total
1. Tattling																					
2. Fighting																					
3. Bullying																					
4. Destroying property																					
5. Cursing																					
6. Sulking																					
7. Arguing																					
8. Uncooperative																					
9. Others																					

INSTRUMENT 8
BEHAVIOR-EVALUATION CHART

	Attempted work	*Followed directions*	*Checked work*	*Did not disturb others*	*Was corrected by teacher*	*Was helpful to others*	*Other good behavior*
Monday							
Tuesday							
Wednesday							
Thursday							
Friday							
Monday							
Tuesday							
Wednesday							
Thursday							
Friday							

INSTRUMENT 9
QUESTIONNAIRE FOR PARENTS OF
FIRST-GRADERS

We, at _____ Elementary School, are trying to evaluate activities that can help children make a happy adjustment to first grade. Please help us by answering the following questions.

	Yes	No
1. The party for preschool children was beneficial to my child.	____	____
2. The party for preschool children helped me as a parent to prepare my child for school.	____	____
3. My child enjoyed the first few days of school.	____	____
4. My child knew the first grade teacher before school started.	____	____
5. My child knew the principal before school started.	____	____
6. My child knew the counselor before school started.	____	____
7. My child was familiar with the school building.	____	____
8. My child had made a friend on the first day of school.	____	____
9. My child has several school friends now.	____	____
10. My child likes school.	____	____

INSTRUMENT 10
QUESTIONNAIRE FOR TRANSFER STUDENTS

Yes No

1. I am glad I attended the "get-acquainted" party at
            (name of school). ___ ___
2. Did you meet the teachers? ___ ___
3. Did you make a school friend on opening day? ___ ___
4. Did you meet the principal? ___ ___
5. Did you meet the counselor? ___ ___
6. Did the party make your first day happier? ___ ___
7. Was it helpful to find out about the location of classrooms, cafeteria, gymnasium, library, and other facilities? ___ ___
8. Did you think that the school was a friendly place? ___ ___
9. Have you now more school friends? ___ ___
10. Do you like _____ School? ___ ___

INSTRUMENT 11
SENTENCE-COMPLETION FORM:
ATTITUDES TOWARD OTHERS

1. Mothers should learn that _____.
2. I wish fathers _____.
3. If I were a parent, I _____.
4. Bus drivers are _____.
5. A father is nice when _____.
6. If only teachers _____.
7. Brothers _____.
8. Sisters _____.
9. People _____.
10. Grandparents are _____.
11. When friends come to visit, my parents _____.
12. When I see the principal, _____.
13. Children _____.
14. When I grow up _____.
15. Baby sitters are _____.
16. People who work in the cafeteria _____.
17. Doctors _____.
18. Cashiers in the grocery store _____.
19. When I try to ask a grown-up a question, _____.
20. Neighbors _____.

INSTRUMENT 12
TEACHER QUESTIONNAIRE

Questionnaire on Guidance Activities and Attitudes

Put a check by the statements with which you agree.

_____ 1. Participation in guidance activities requires too much of my time.

_____ 2. Because of the guidance program, I now have a better understanding of the students.

_____ 3. Student failure is never the teacher's fault.

_____ 4. I now observe students more carefully.

_____ 5. There are probably few beneficial results from the guidance program.

_____ 6. My knowledge of students' conditions has not been increased by guidance activities.

_____ 7. Once a teacher finds a good teaching technique, he or she should not change it.

_____ 8. I have developed new ideas in classroom management from guidance activities.

_____ 9. Guidance workshops are usually not very useful to me.

_____ 10. The wants of children are as important as the wants of adults.

_____ 11. Poor students ask too many questions.

_____ 12. Children's individual needs make little difference in classroom teaching.

_____ 13. School guidance programs are not of much use.

_____ 14. Different children have different needs at different times.

_____ 15. New teaching techniques and devices make my job more interesting.

_____ 16. Special students require too much time.

_____ 17. Slow learners provide a challenge for me.

_____ 18. The guidance program gives me an opportunity to use new techniques and materials.

_____ 19. Because of guidance activities I am more alert to the needs of my students.

_____ 20. Laziness is the only reason for low achievement.

_____ 21. Children seldom enjoy attending school.

INSTRUMENT 13
STUDY-HABITS SURVEY (A)

	Never	Some- times	Always
1. Do you keep a schedule of the time you plan to spend each day studying?	____	____	____
2. Do you divide your time among the different subjects to be studied?	____	____	____
3. Do you spread the study time over at least five days of the week?	____	____	____
4. Do you keep up to date in your homework?	____	____	____
5. Do you study in a place where you are away from interferences such as talking, radio, or TV?	____	____	____
6. When you study, do you have all the materials you need?	____	____	____
7. Do you write down your school assignments?	____	____	____
8. Do you ask for help when you have a problem with your homework?	____	____	____
9. Do you make up a sample test for yourself and try to answer it?	____	____	____
10. Do you budget your time?	____	____	____

INSTRUMENT 14
STUDY-HABITS SURVEY (B)

	Yes	No	Some-times
1. Do you follow a daily schedule plan?	___	___	___
2. Are you well organized and do you have everything you need when you sit down to study?	___	___	___
3. Do you use your time wisely?	___	___	___
4. Do you write down your assignments when they are given to you?	___	___	___
5. Are your notebooks neat and well organized?	___	___	___
6. Do you hand in your assignments on time?	___	___	___
7. Do you avoid putting off long-range assignments such as term papers or special reports until the last minute?	___	___	___
8. Is your written work neat and easy to read?	___	___	___
9. Do you go over tests and assignments when they are returned and learn from your mistakes?	___	___	___
10. Do you begin to study for a test a few days in advance rather than wait until the night before?	___	___	___
11. Do you participate in class activities and discussions?	___	___	___
12. Do you ask your teacher for help when you don't understand something?	___	___	___

INSTRUMENT 15
CAREER-AWARENESS INVENTORY (A)

Are the following statements true (T) or false (F)?

_____ 1. I can do any work I choose.

_____ 2. I am the only "me" in the world.

_____ 3. People have different abilities.

_____ 4. School is my work responsibility.

_____ 5. Money is the only thing to consider when choosing a job.

_____ 6. One's interests are important when looking into various kinds of work.

_____ 7. All jobs require the same skills.

_____ 8. All jobs are important.

_____ 9. My schoolwork will be important in getting a job.

_____ 10. All jobs require a college education.

_____ 11. The way people feel about their work is not important.

Complete the following statements.

12. Most of the parents of the students at _____ School work in _____.

13. Name a job you would like to have. _____

14. List three skills that are needed for that job.

_____

_____

15. List three school subjects that would be useful in that job.

_____

_____

16. The job your parents would like for you to have is_____.

17. The largest industry in _____ is _____.

18. The two largest businesses in _____ are

_____

19. Name a place where you would like to work. _____

20. List three skills needed in that place of work.

_____

_____

21. List three skills needed to be a good homemaker.

_____

_____

22. List two types of jobs that people do in this school.

_____

_____

23. Name the most important job in the world. _____
24. Why do we have jobs? _____
_____

INSTRUMENT 16
CAREER-AWARENESS INVENTORY (B)

Name of student _____

1. Name the different classes offered in the local vocational school that provide vocational training.

_____
_____
_____
_____

2. Name two jobs concerned with parks and forests.

_____

3. Name five jobs that deal mainly with people.

_____
_____
_____
_____

4. Name five jobs that deal with things.

_____
_____
_____
_____

5. Name five jobs that deal with ideas.

_____
_____
_____
_____

INSTRUMENT 17
CAREER-AWARENESS INVENTORY (LOCAL)

1. List the five major industries in the _____ area.

_____

_____

_____

_____

_____

2. What type of work is done in each industry? What are their products?

_____   _____

_____   _____

_____   _____

_____   _____

_____   _____

3. Which industry employs the most people? _____

4. Which industry pays the highest wages? _____

5. Which industries require special training for their employees?

_____

6. Where does your father work? _____

7. What type of work does your father do? _____

8. Where does your mother work? _____

9. What type of work does your mother do? _____

10. Which industry is closest to your home? _____

11. Which is the oldest industry in your town? _____

INSTRUMENT 18
INTEREST-INVENTORY QUESTIONNAIRE

	Yes	No
1. The inventory made me aware of some interests I didn't know I had.	___	___
2. The inventory was fun to take.	___	___
3. The inventory will help me work harder at some of my subjects.	___	___
4. The inventory will help me decide what subjects to take in junior high school.	___	___
5. The small-group discussions with people who have my same interests made me feel good.	___	___
6. The small-group discussions with people whose interests are different from mine helped me understand how people feel about things in which they are interested and I am not.	___	___

NAME INDEX

SUBJECT INDEX

ACTIVITIES INDEX